Decorative
Cross-Stitch Alphabets

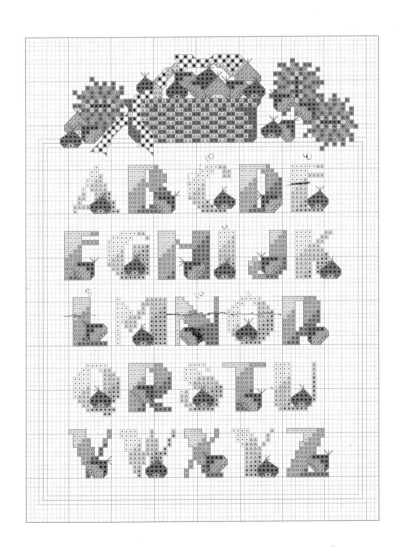

Sterling Publishing Co., Inc.
New York

Editor-in-chief: *Cristina Sperandeo*
Sketches by *Michele Corriga*
Taken from *Speciale Punto Croce*
Translated by *Studio Queens*

Thread color numbers refer to DMC embroidery floss

Library of Congress Cataloging-in-Publication Data Available

10   9   8   7   6 5   4   3   2   1

Published by Sterling Publishing Company, Inc.
387 Park Avenue South, New York, NY 10016
First published in Italy by RCS Libri S.p.A.
under the title *La Biblioteca del Punto Croce—Alfabeti*
© 1999 RCS Libri S.p.A., Milan 1st Edition Great Fabbri Manuals April 1999
© 2001 English translation by Sterling Publishing Co., Inc.
Distributed in Canada by Sterling Publishing Co., Inc.
c/o Canadian Manda Group, One Atlantic Avenue, Suite 105
Toronto, Onatario, Canada M6K 3E7
Distributed in Great Britain and Europe by Cassell PLC
Wellington House, 125 Strand, London WC2R 0BB, England
Distributed in Australia by Capricorn Link (Australia) Pty Ltd.
P.O. Box 704, Windsor, NSW 2756, Australia
Printed in China

Sterling ISBN 0-8069-7603-9

CONTENTS

BUNNIES

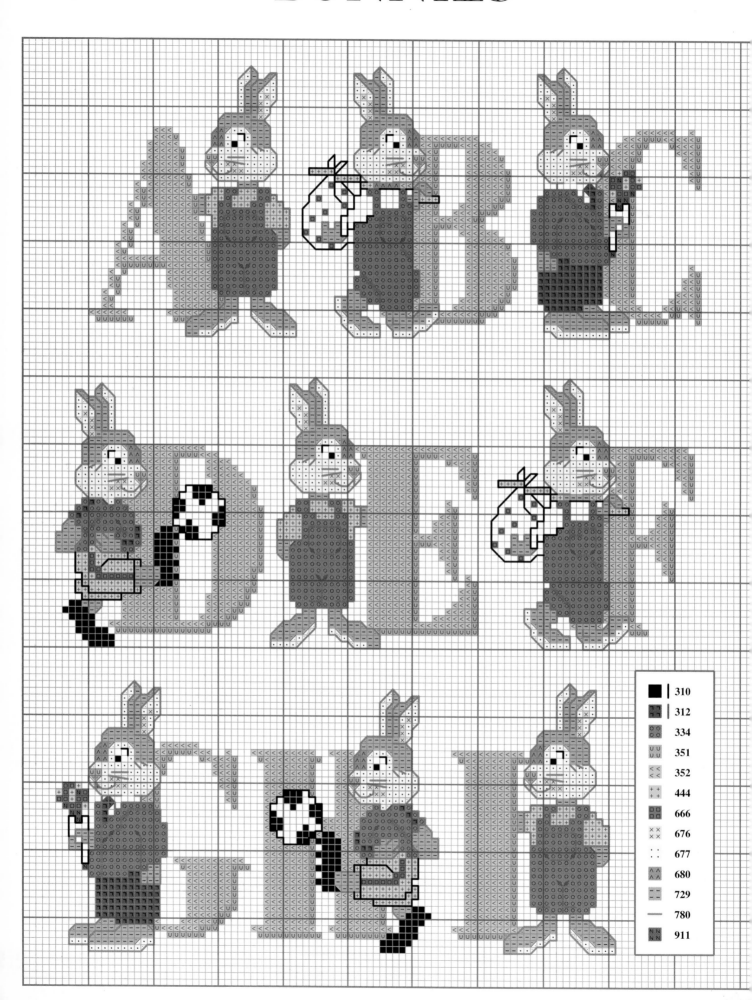

■ │	310
▧ │	312
⊙⊙	334
∪∪	351
<<	352
++	444
▣▣	666
××	676
∶∶	677
∧∧	680
⁻⁻	729
—	780
N N	911

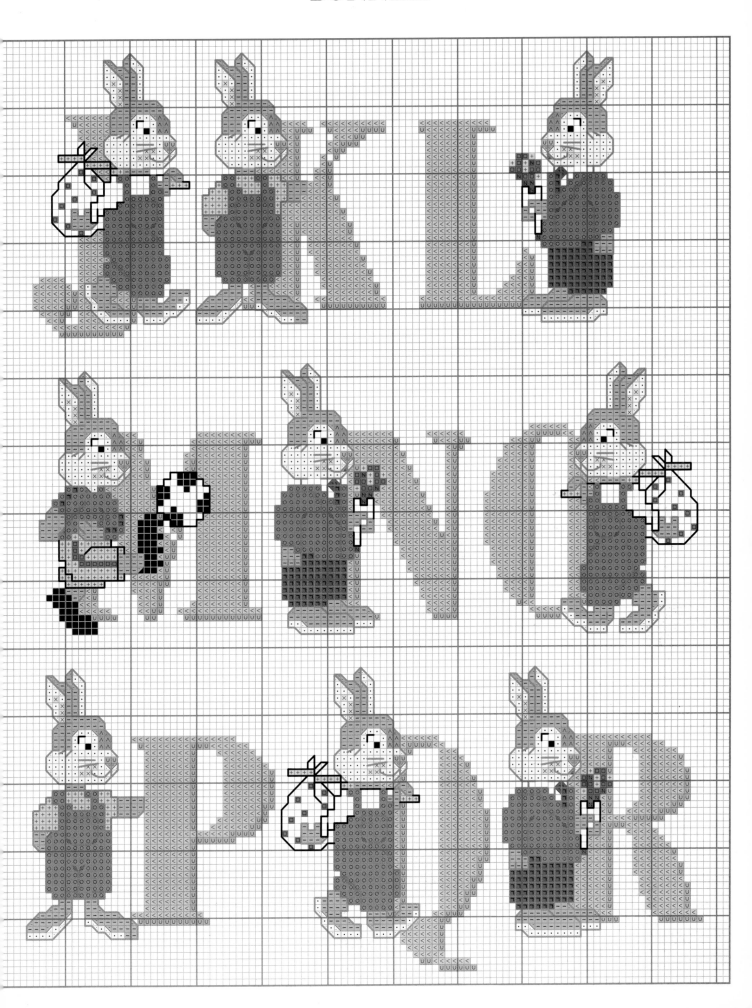

BUNNIES

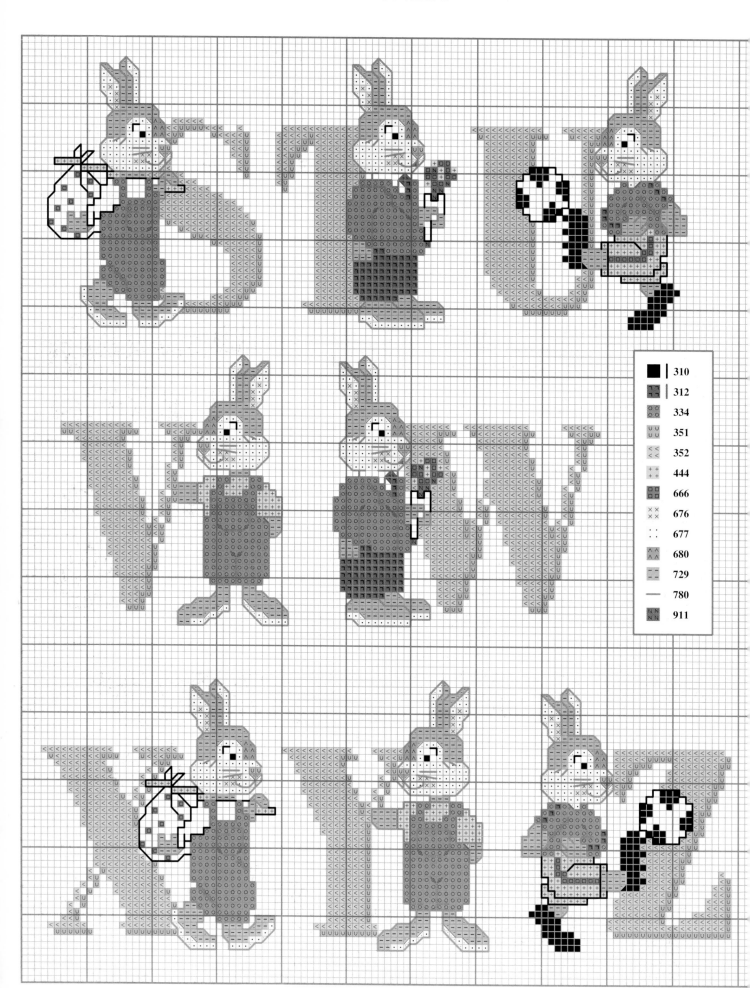

■	310
⊐⊓	312
⊙⊙	334
UU	351
<<	352
++	444
⊞⊞	666
××	676
∶∶	677
∧∧	680
⊡⊡	729
—	780
NN	911

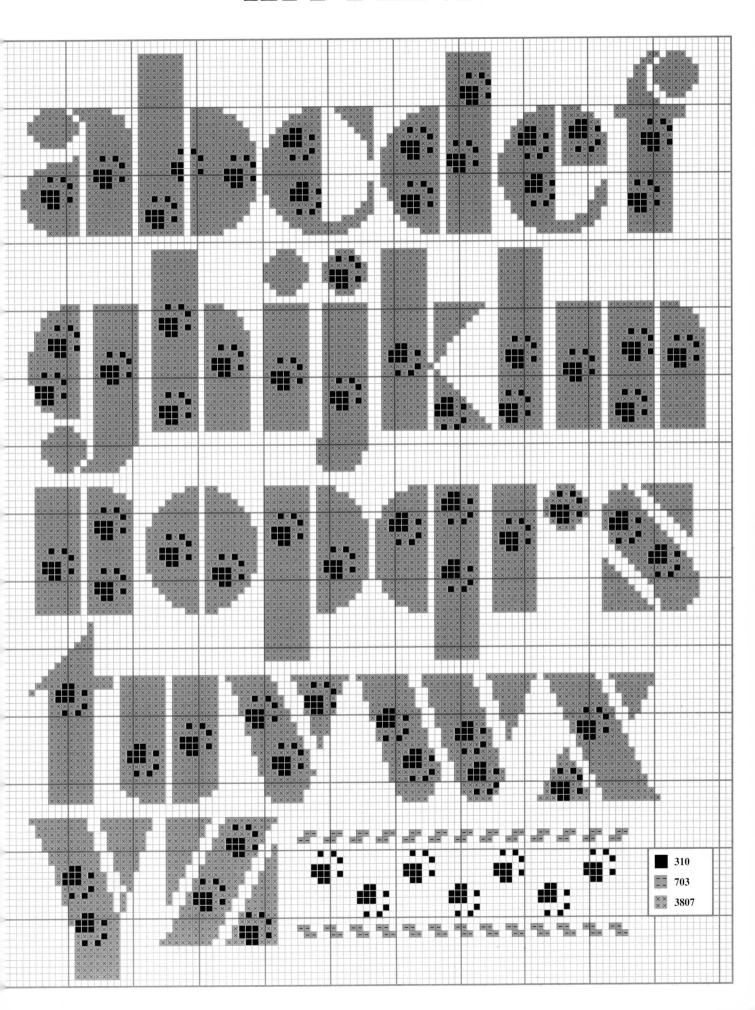

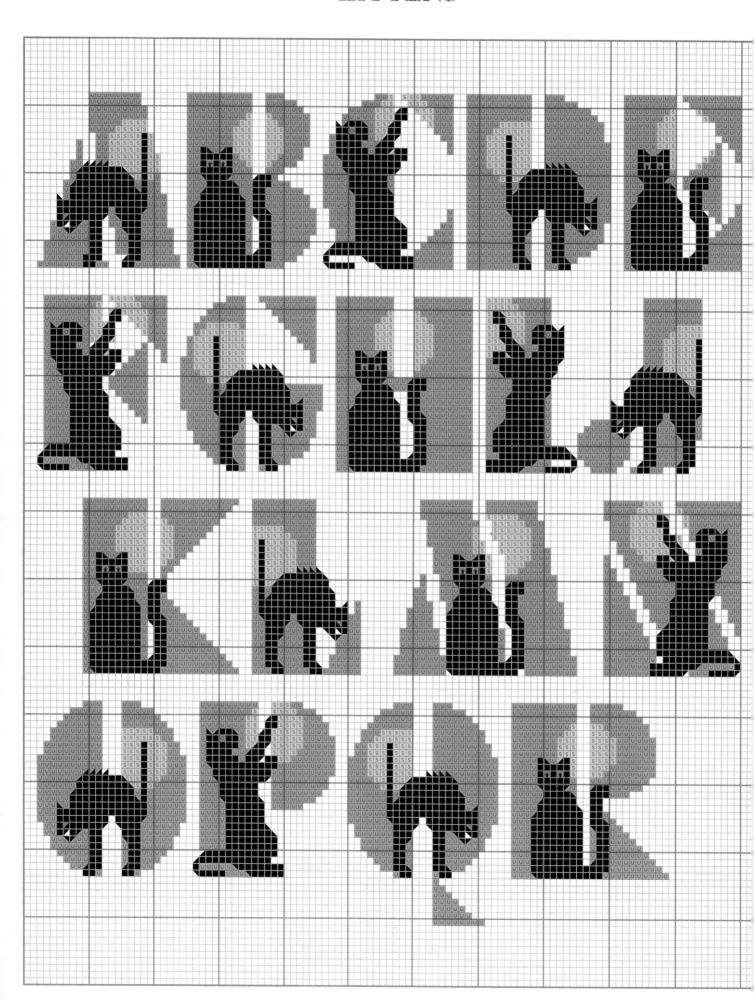

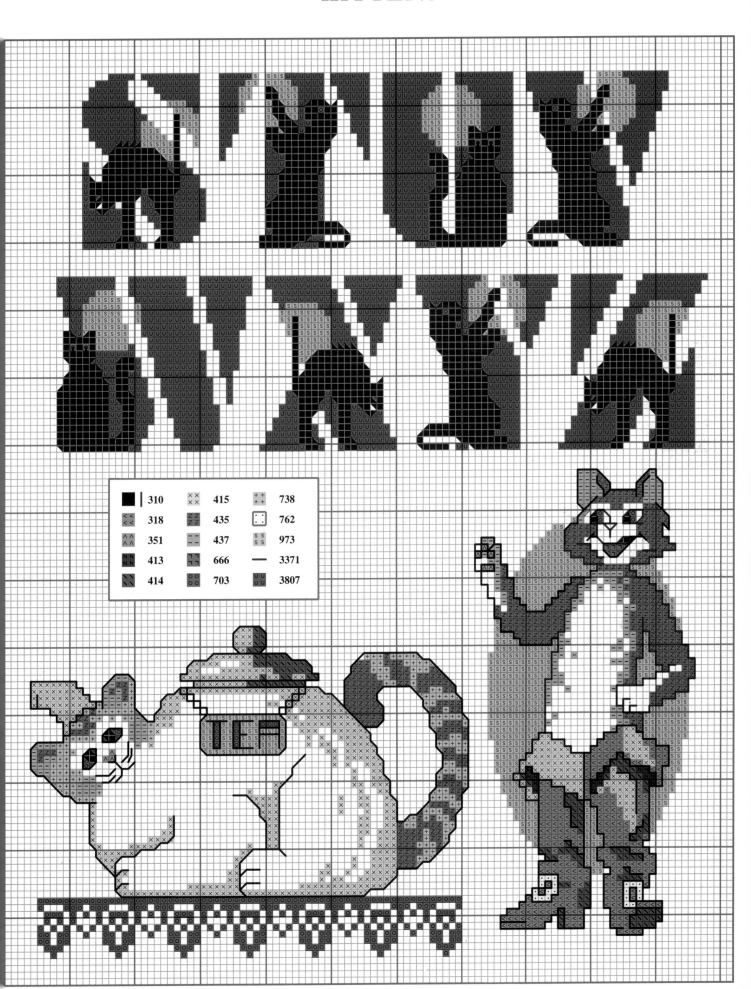

	310	××	415	++	738
<<	318	zz	435	⠂⠂	762
^^	351	--	437	ss	973
NN	413	⌐⌐	666	—	3371
⫽⫽	414	oo	703	UU	3807

HORSES

—	310
s s s	402
U U U	414
+ + +	415
	444
—	666
—	699
	701
o o	720
< <	721
z z	780
△ △	782
- -	783
	898
	938
	3031
□ □	3032
↑ ↑	3033
	3371

ARCHITECTURE

—	310
	318
	414
✗ ✗	415
—	470
+ +	762
	3712

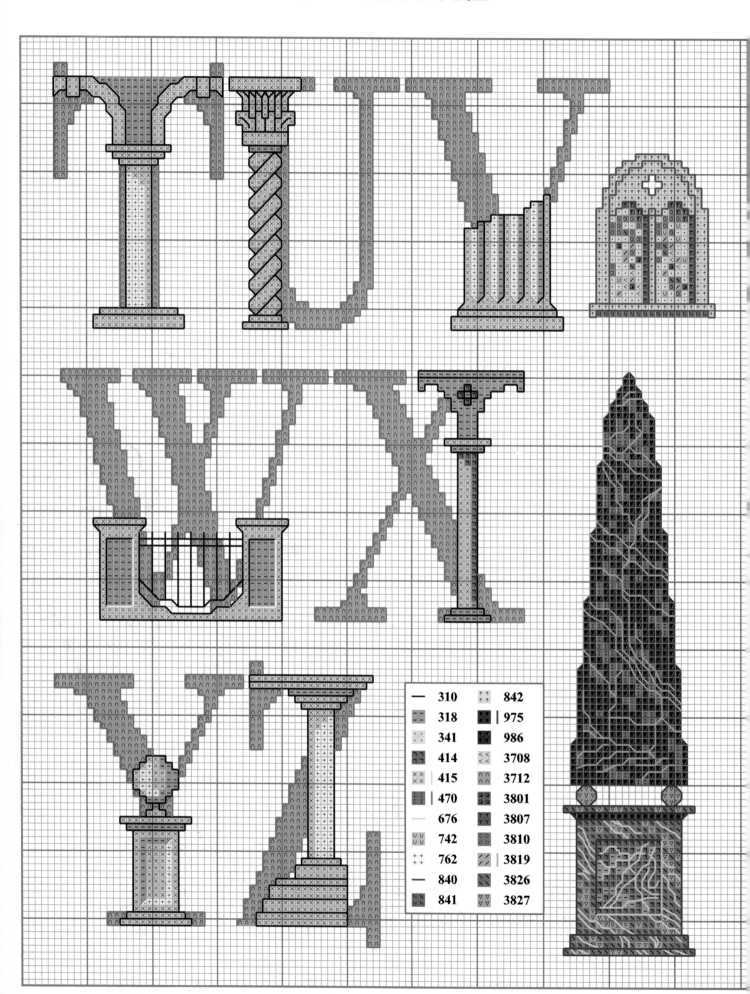

—	310	↑↑	842
▦	318		975
∴	341		986
▦	414	<<	3708
××	415	∩∩	3712
▤	470	▦	3801
—	676	▦	3807
∪∪	742	○○	3810
++	762	⁄⁄	3819
—	840	▦	3826
NN	841	▽▽	3827

MUSIC

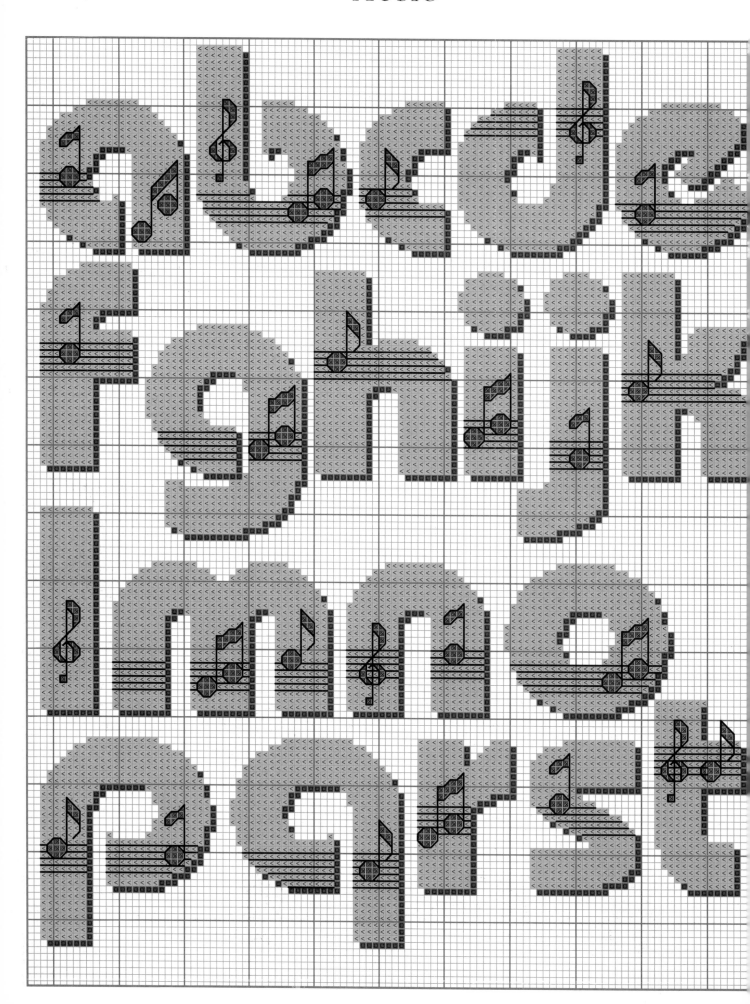

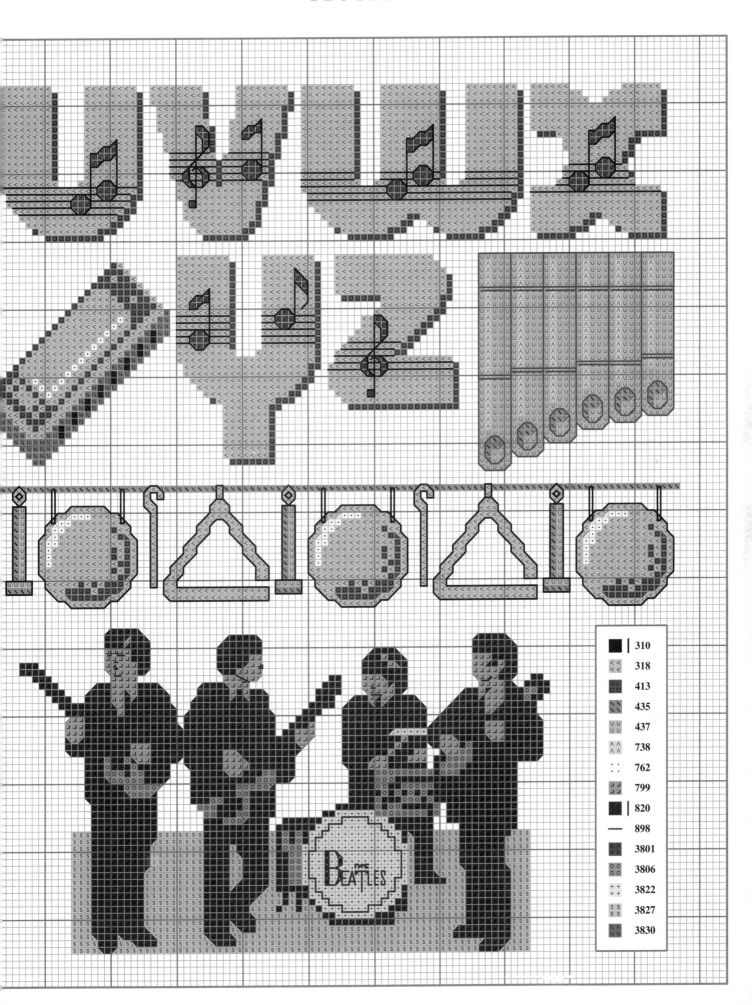

SNOW-CAPPED MOUNTAINS

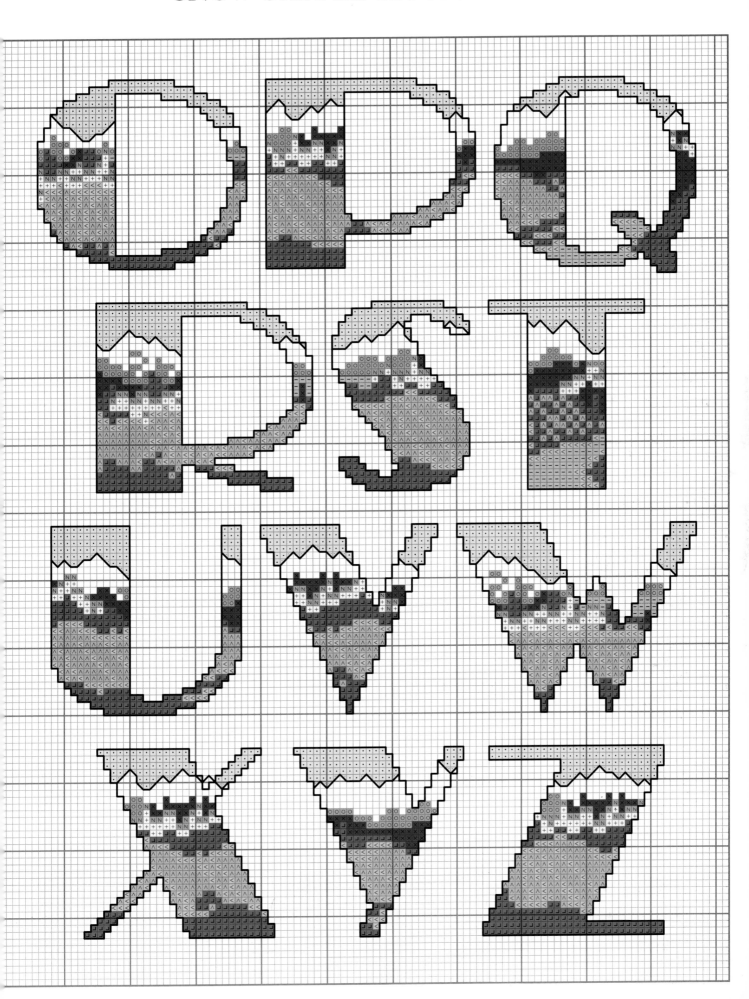

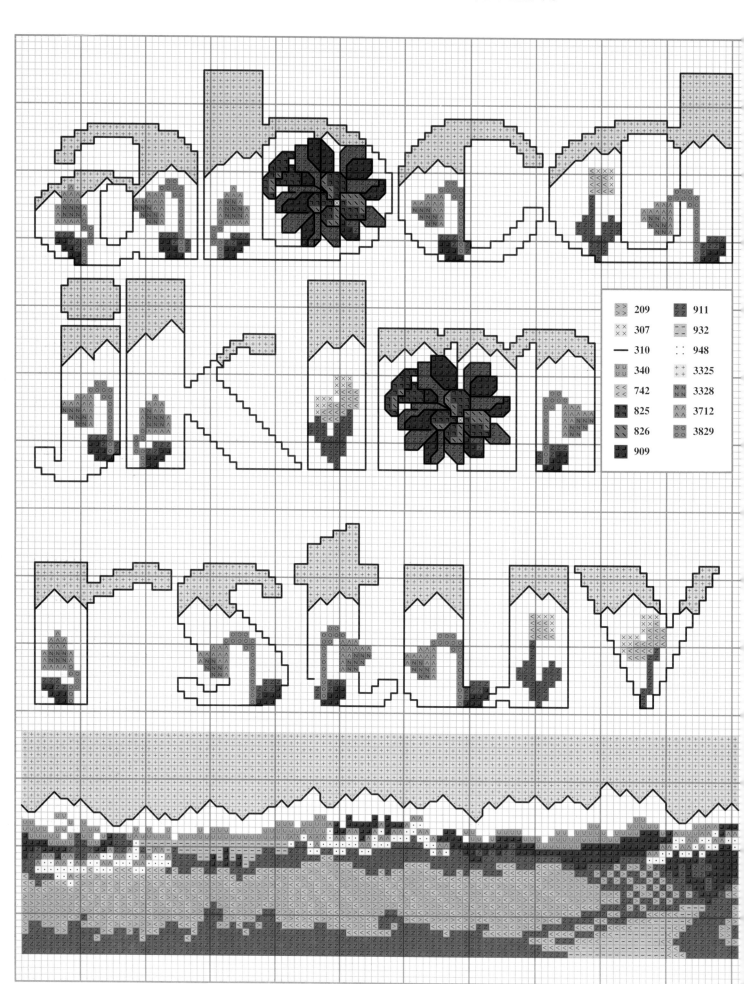

>>	209	ZZ	911
XX	307	--	932
—	310	::	948
UU	340	++	3325
<<	742	NN	3328
	825	^^	3712
	826	OO	3829
	909		

HOLLY

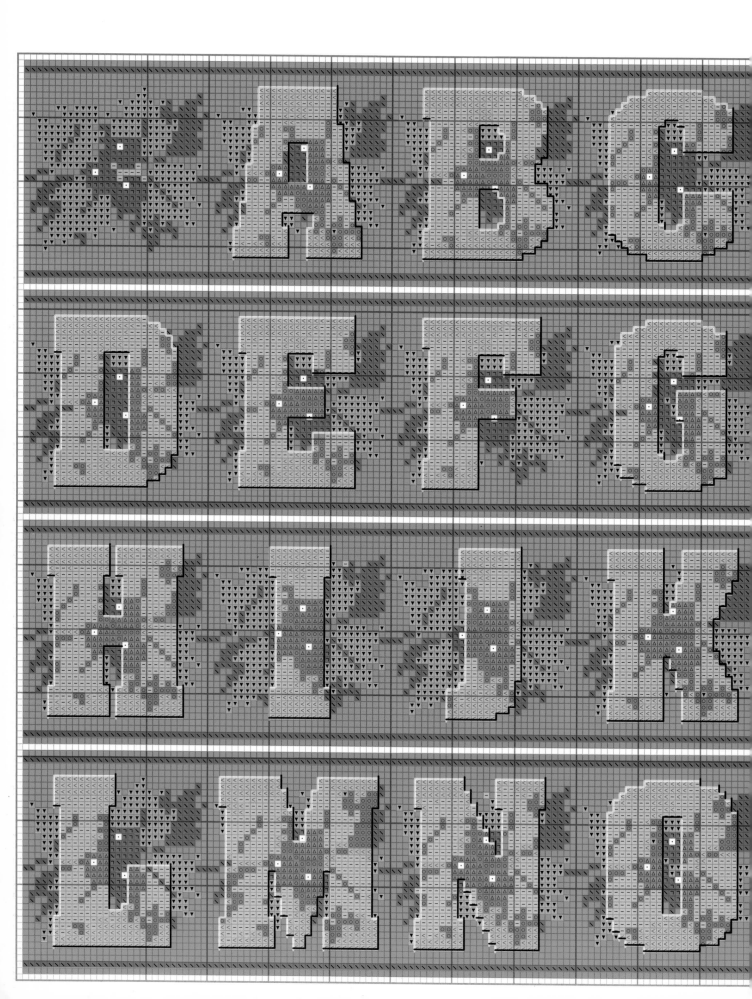

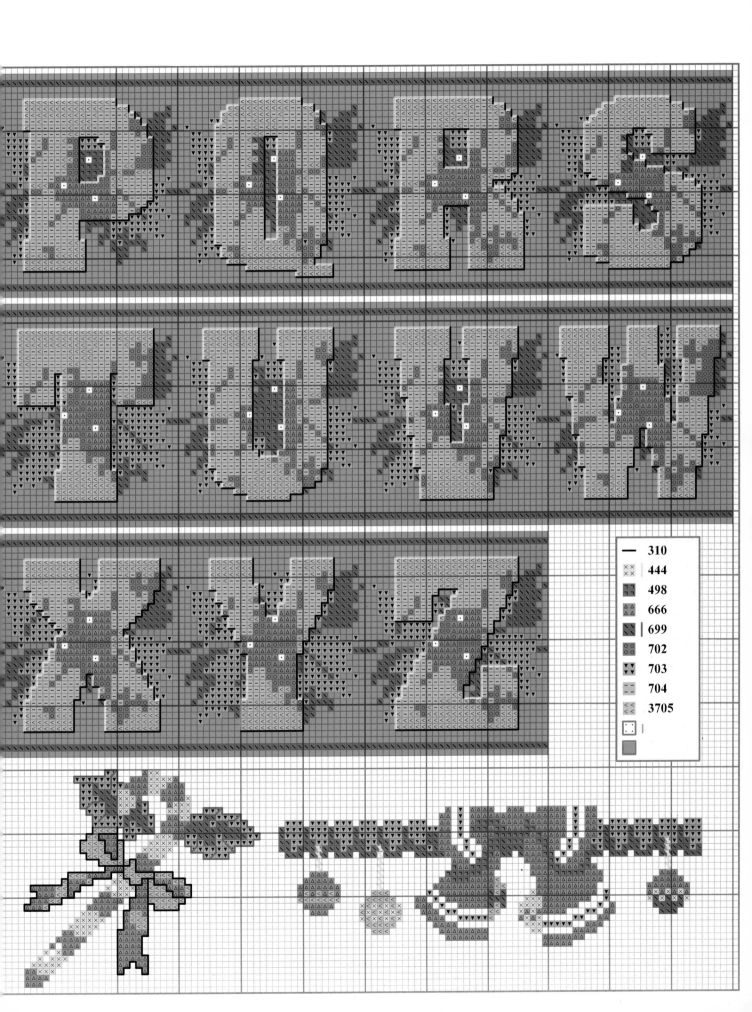

—	310
××	444
◪◪	498
▵▵	666
◩◩	699
⊙⊙	702
▼▼	703
--	704
<<	3705
⬚	
▦	

■ | 310	○○	702
⌐⌐ 321	≪≪	703
×× 444	∪∪	781
NN 666	⌐⌐	783
◥◥ 699	++	970

SANTA CLAUS

∴	
■	310
⊡	321
⧄	606
▨	840
«	3708
⬚	3818
∩	3829

CHRISTMAS BALLS

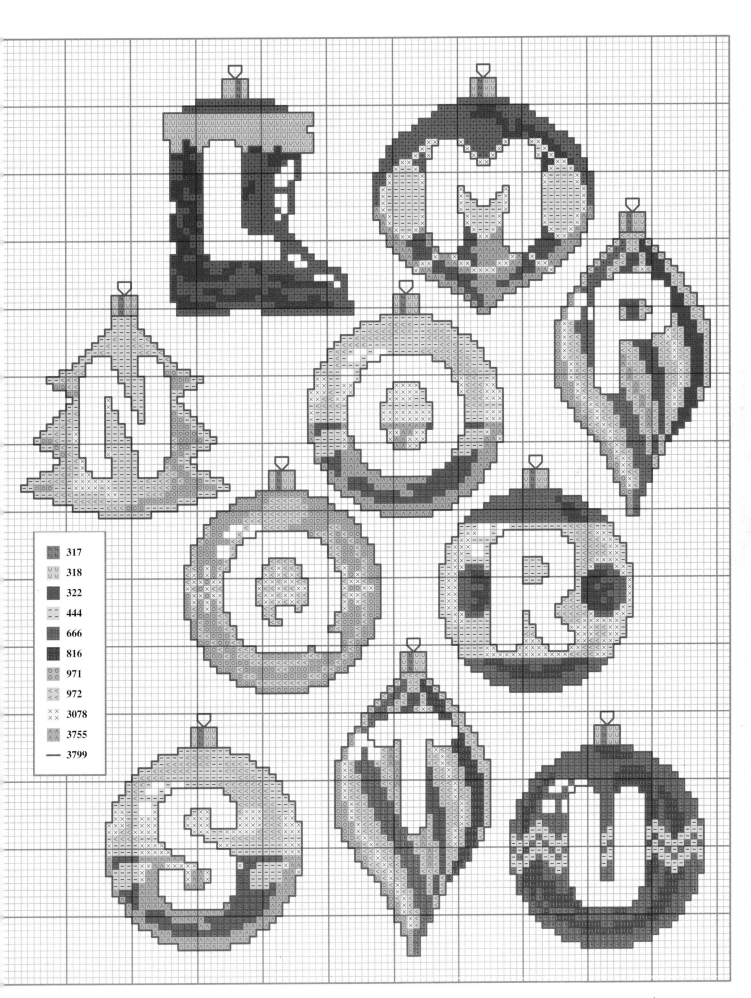

N N / N	317
U U / U	318
	322
– – / –	444
	666
	816
o o / o	971
< < / <	972
x x / x	3078
^ ^ / ^	3755
—	3799

■ |	310	oo	906
▨	317	<<	907
‖	318	◪ |	935
▨	322	^^	971
××	353	⊡	972
++	444	∴	3078
▨	666	⁼⁼	3706
▨	816	UU	3755
▨	904	—	3799
ᴢᴢ	905		

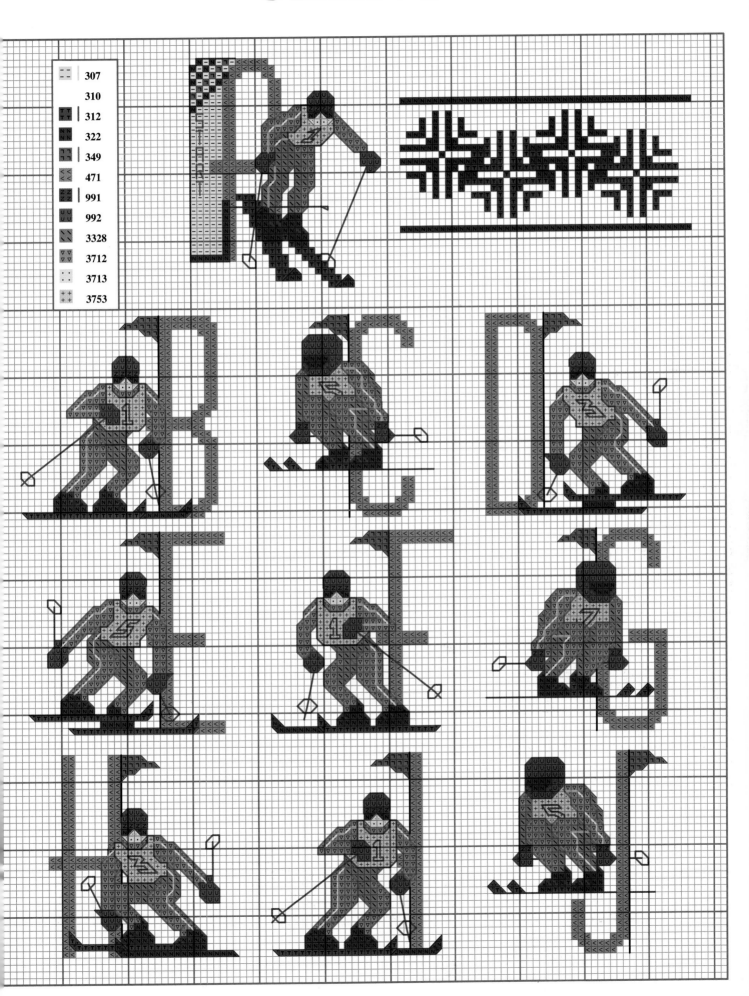

∷	307
	310
T	312
N	322
⊟	349
≪	471
Z	991
U	992
∖	3328
▽	3712
∷	3713
+	3753

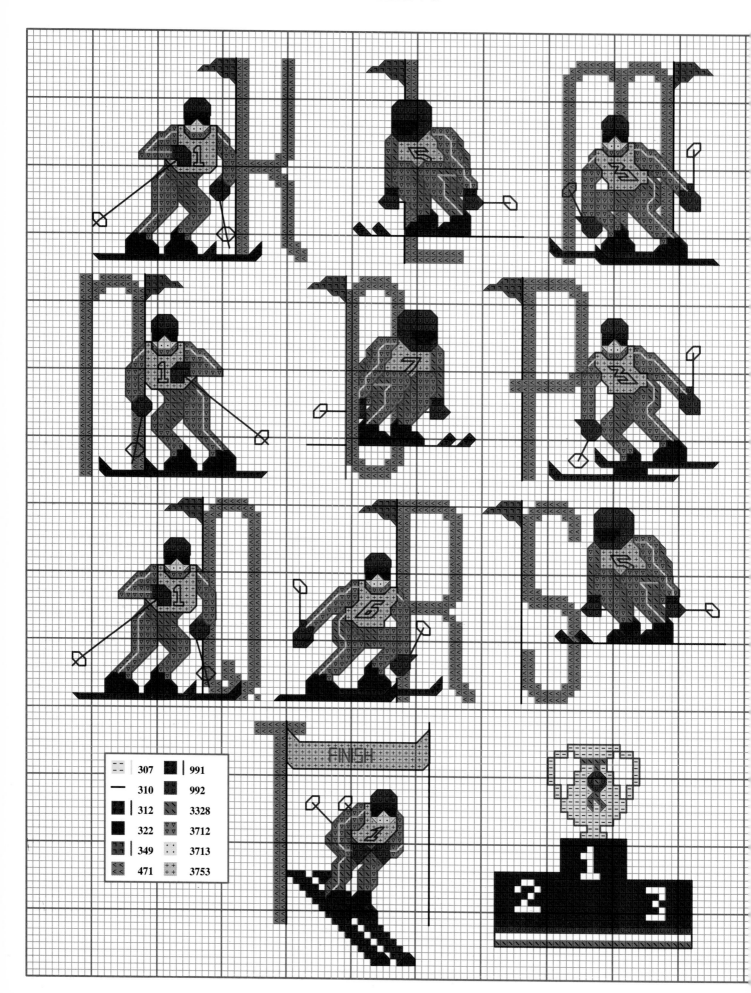

	307		991
	310		992
	312		3328
	322		3712
	349		3713
	471		3753

FINSH

1
2
3

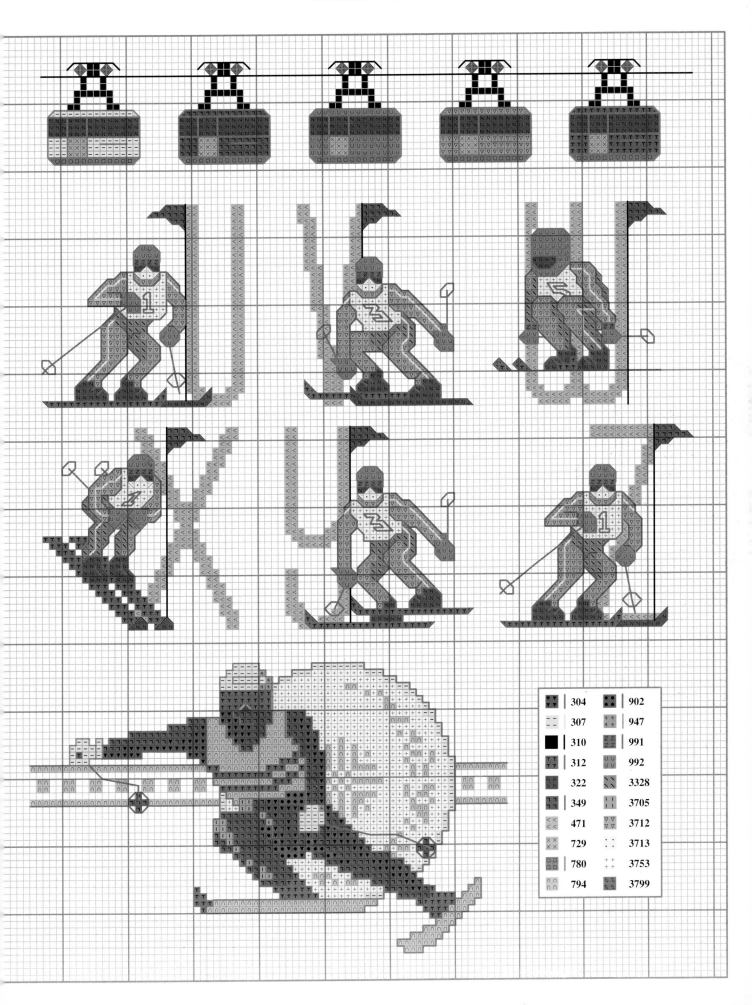

▼▼	304	••	902
— —	307	4 4	947
■	310	Z Z	991
T T	312	U U	992
	322	⫽ ⫽	3328
	349	I I	3705
< <	471	▽▽	3712
X X	729	∶∶	3713
□□	780	++	3753
⨅⨅	794	◣◣	3799

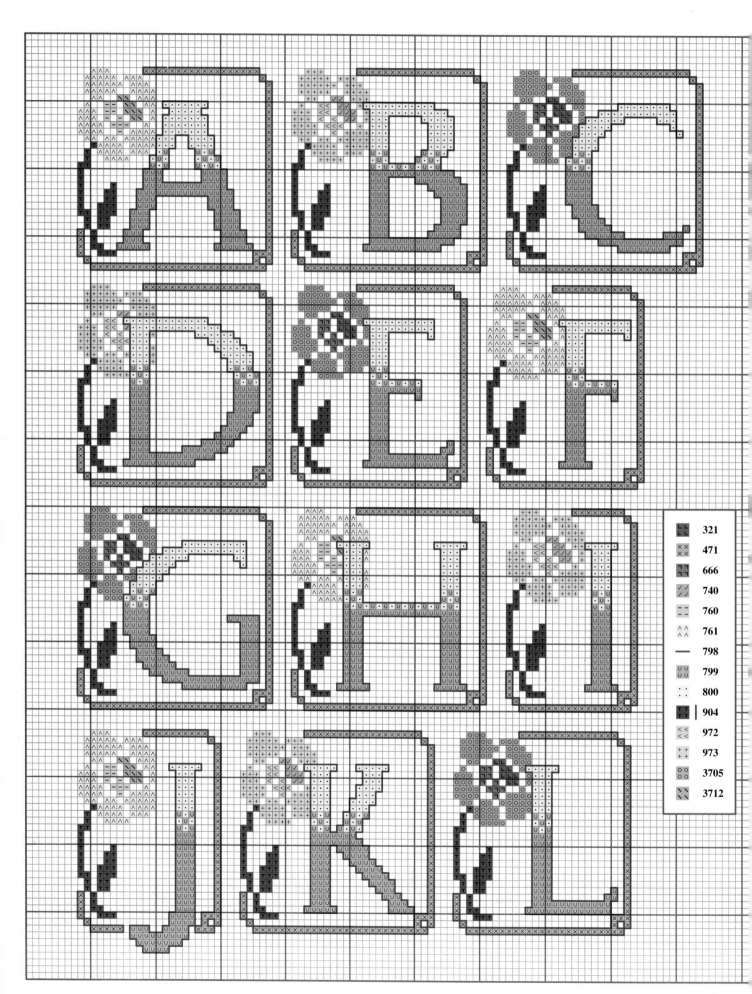

⊥⊥	321	
XX	471	
ᴦᴦ	666	
✓✓	740	
=−	760	
∧∧	761	
—	798	
∪∪	799	
∷	800	
∎ ∣	904	
<<	972	
++	973	
⊙⊙	3705	
⍀⍀	3712	

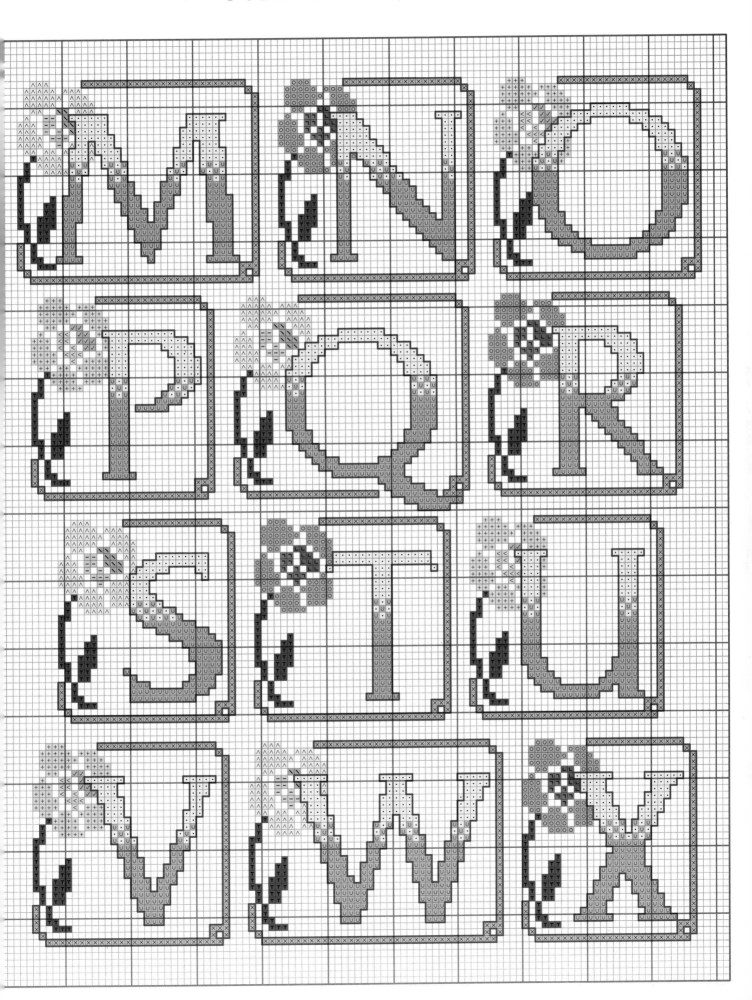

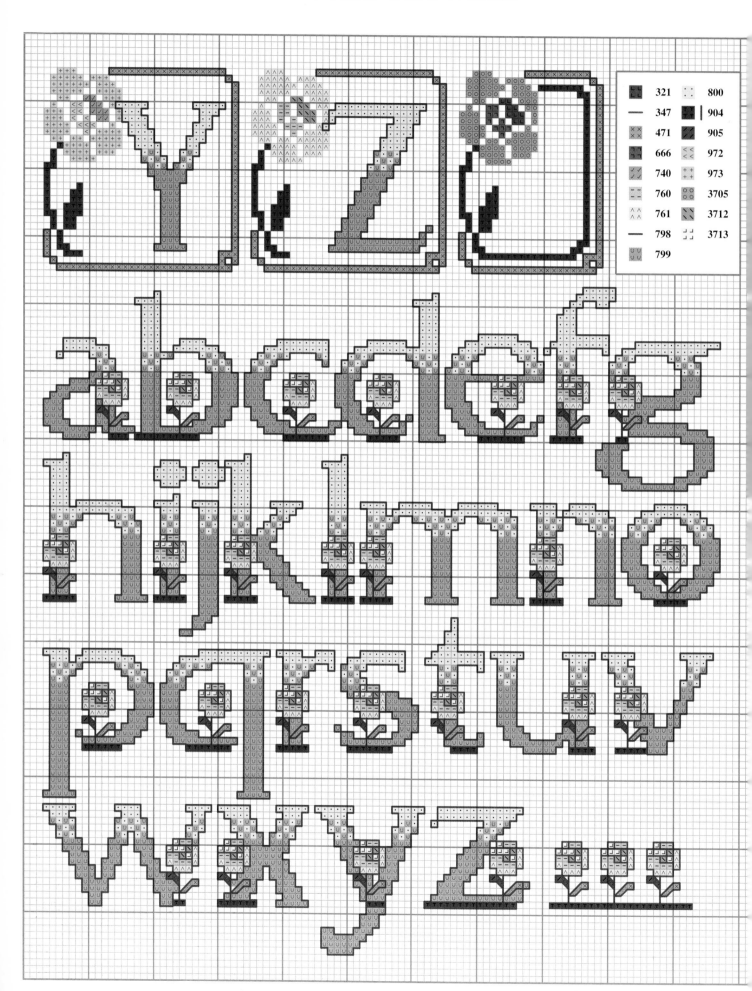

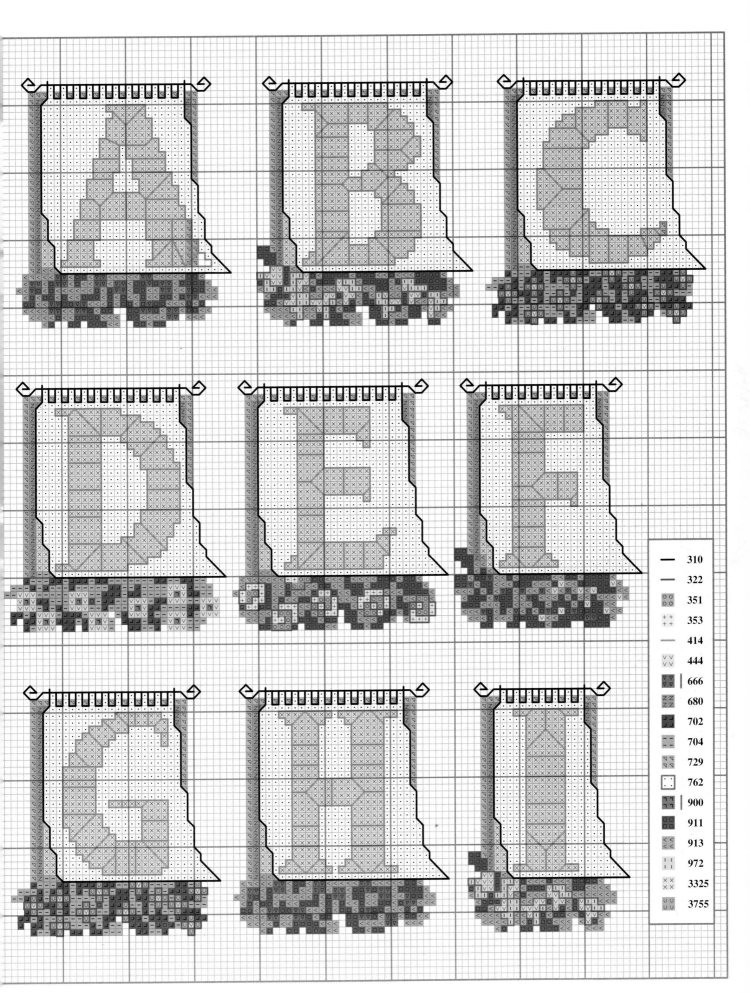

—	310
—	322
o o	351
+ +	353
—	414
v v	444
⊽⊽ |	666
z z	680
■	702
- -	704
⊓⊓	729
∴	762
⊓⊓ |	900
⊡	911
< <	913
¦¦	972
× ×	3325
∪∪	3755

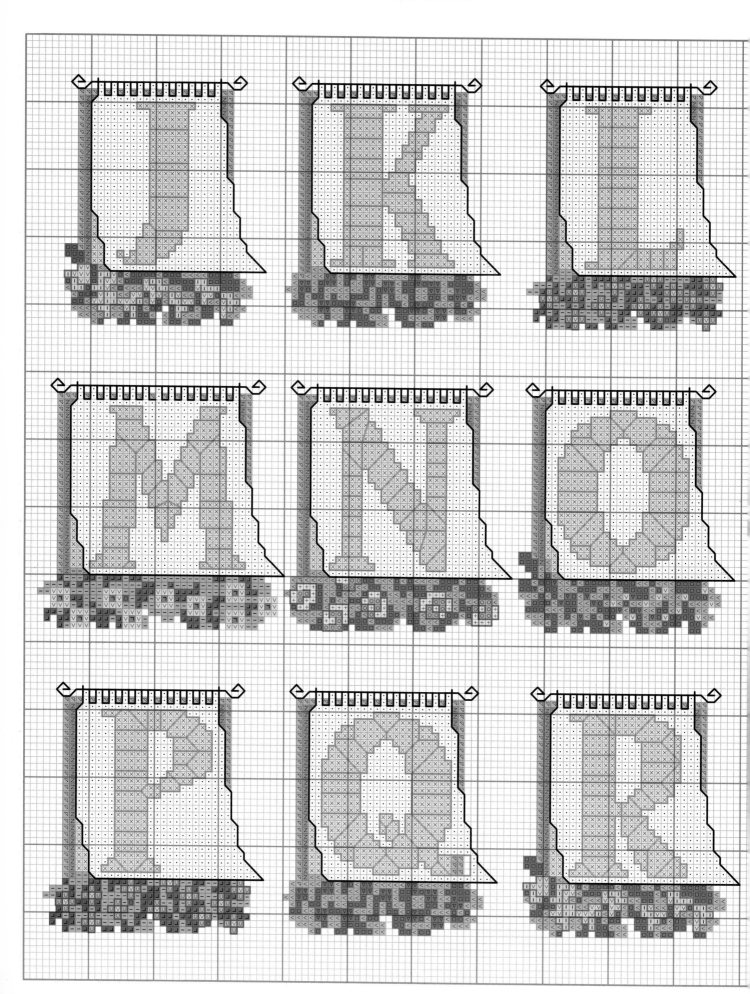

—	310	⊐⊐	704
—	322	⊿⊿	729
oo	351	⊡	762
++	353	⊏⊏ |	900
—	414	⊟⊟	911
vv	444	<<	913
▽▽ |	666	ıı	972
zz	680	xx	3325
⊔⊔	702	⊔⊔	3755

SPRING

—	312	TT	780
351	351	VV	782
352	352	II	783
444	444	—	817
517	517	—	829
ZZ	518	946	946
UU	519	II	972
699	699	<<	3325
702	702	✓✓	3328
703	703	SS	3348
==	725	3712	3712
∷	747	→→	3713
760	760	OO	3755
++	761	XX	3761

■	310	○○ ○○	741
—	350	<< <<	743
□□ □□	351	‖ ‖	794
∪∪ ∪∪	352	ss ss	813
- - - -	353	↘↘ ↘↘	817
∨∨ ∨∨	517	++ ++	827
×× ××	677	⊞⊟	904
↘↘ ↘↘	729	zz zz	906
TT TT	740	∧∧ ∧∧	996

EASTER RIBBONS

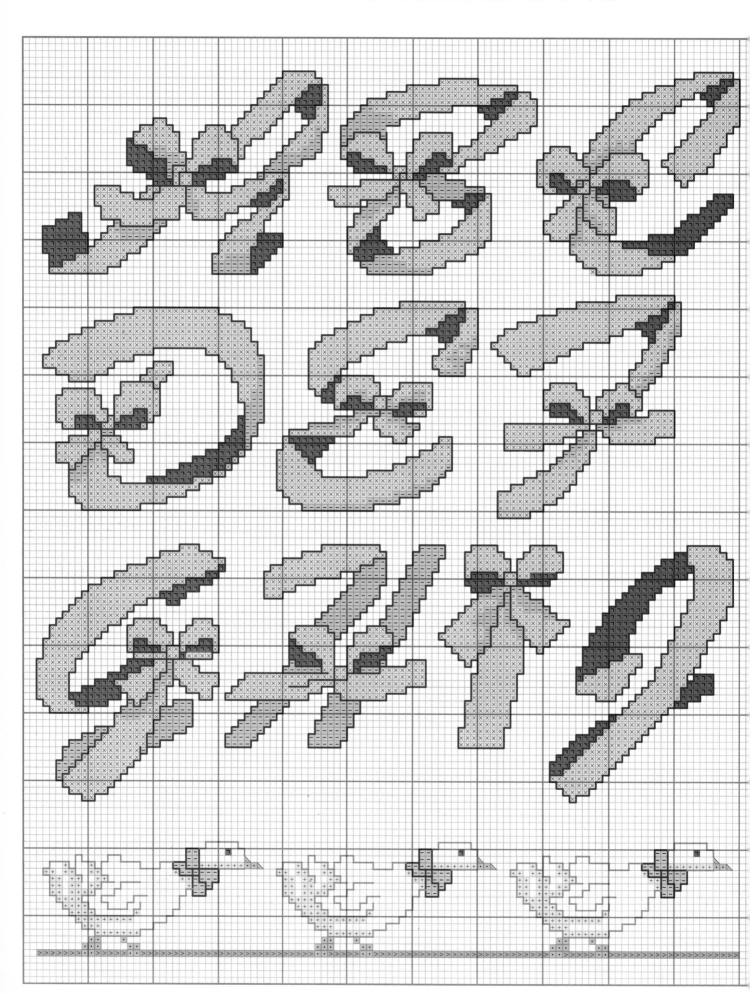

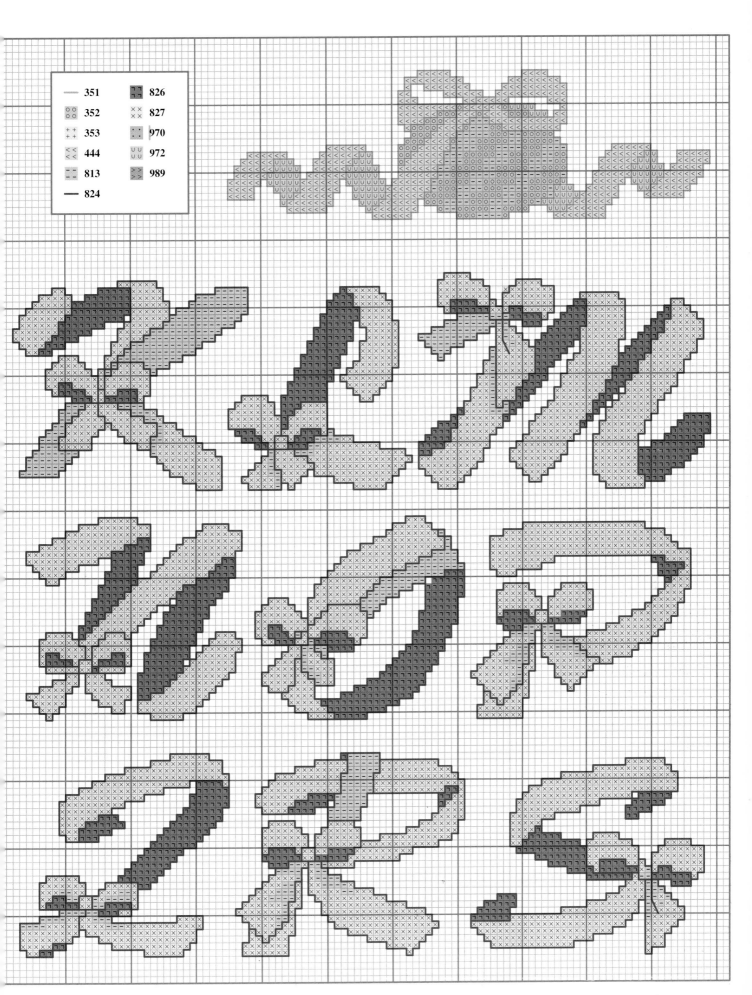

	351		813
	352		815
	353		824
	470		826
	471		827
	666		948
	742		

PRESENTS

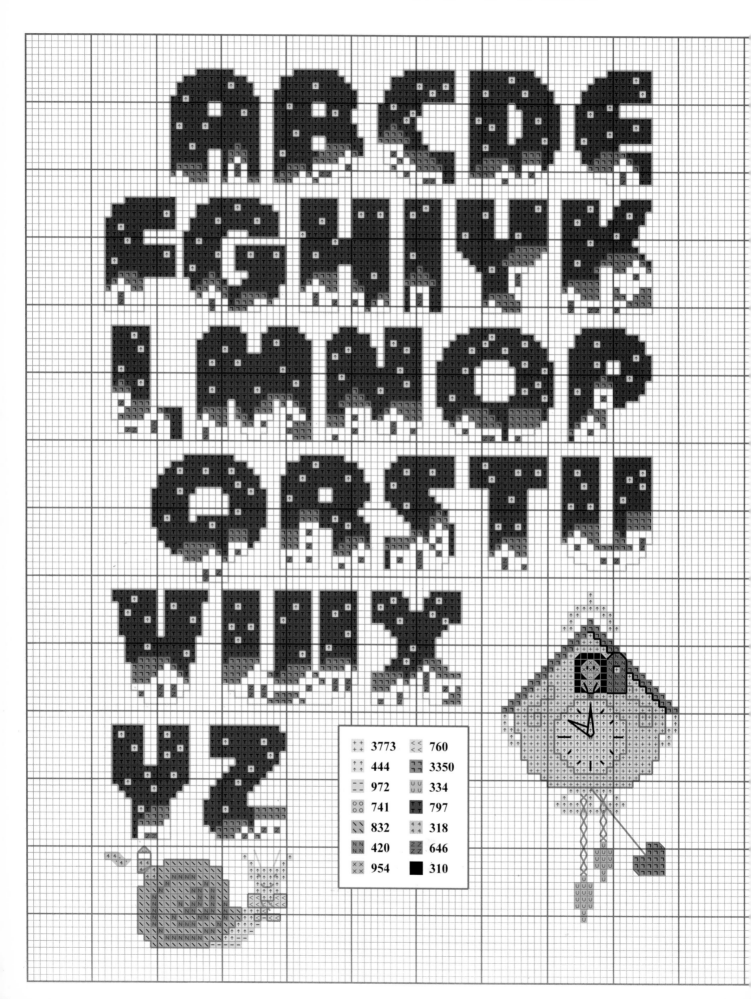

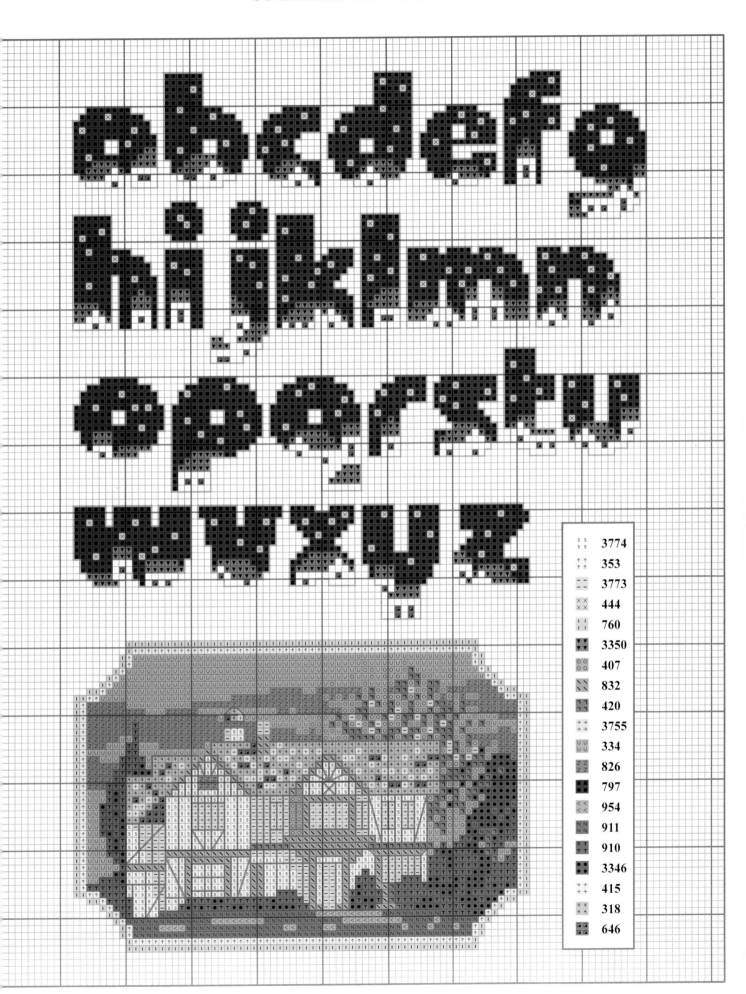

s s s s	3774
↑ ↑ ↑ ↑	353
‒ ‒ ‒ ‒	3773
✕ ✕ ✕ ✕	444
┆ ┆ ┆ ┆	760
▼▼ ▼▼	3350
◦◦ ◦◦	407
N N N N	832
⌐ ⌐ ⌐ ⌐	420
→ → → →	3755
U U U U	334
Z Z Z Z	826
■■ ■■	797
< < < <	954
N N N N	911
T T T T	910
●● ●●	3346
✛ ✛ ✛ ✛	415
◢◢ ◢◢	318
◳◳ ◳◳	646

ANTIQUE FURNITURE

—	310
T T T T	414
	445
—	470
X X X X	472
▢ ▢ ▢ ▢	676
—	740
U U U U	742
S S S S	772
—	840
—	3687
✓ ✓ ✓ ✓	3706
< < < <	3708
4 4 4 4	3819
I I I I	3820
+ + + +	3823
⋅ ⋅ ⋅ ⋅	3827
—	3829

▬	310
Z Z Z	318
+ +	341
▬	414
^ ^	444
N N N	470
X X	676
U U U	742
▪▪	840
▬	3687
s s s	3756
✓ ✓	3706
< <	3708
▼ ▼	3807
◂ ◂	3819
↑ ↑	3823
∴ ∴	3827
▦ ▦	3829

318		975	
414	—	3689	↑↑
415	△△	3755	−
444	✕✕	3706	✓✓
445	s s	3708	<<
470	z z	3819	++
472	++	3820	U U
606	▼▼	3826	⌐⌐
676	—	3827	∴∴
840	●●	3829	N N

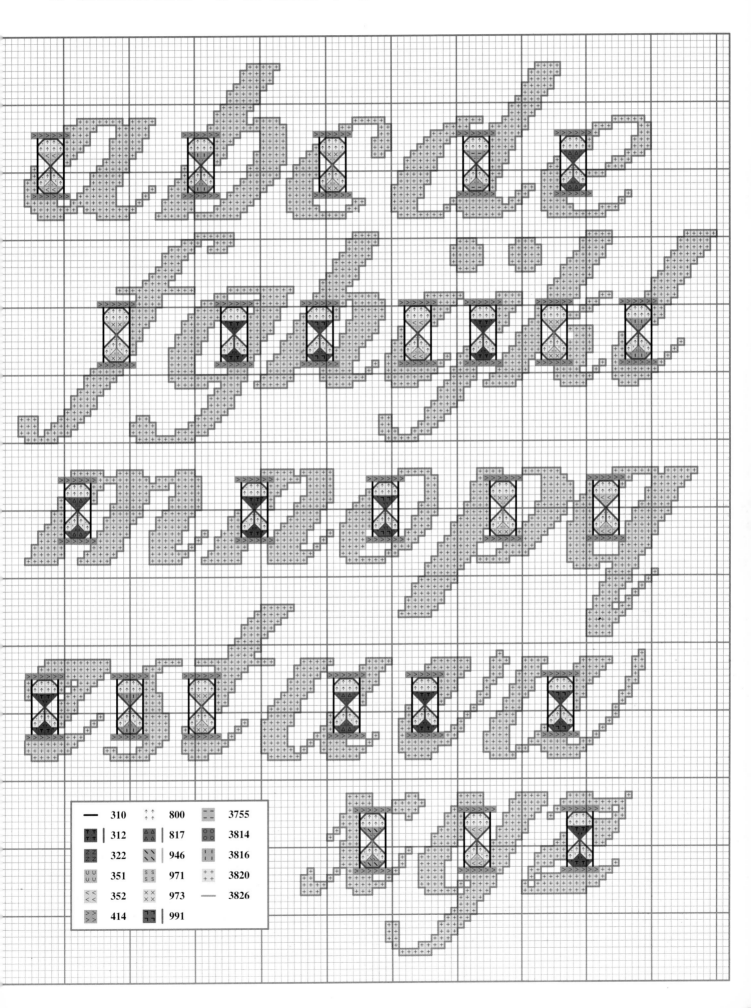

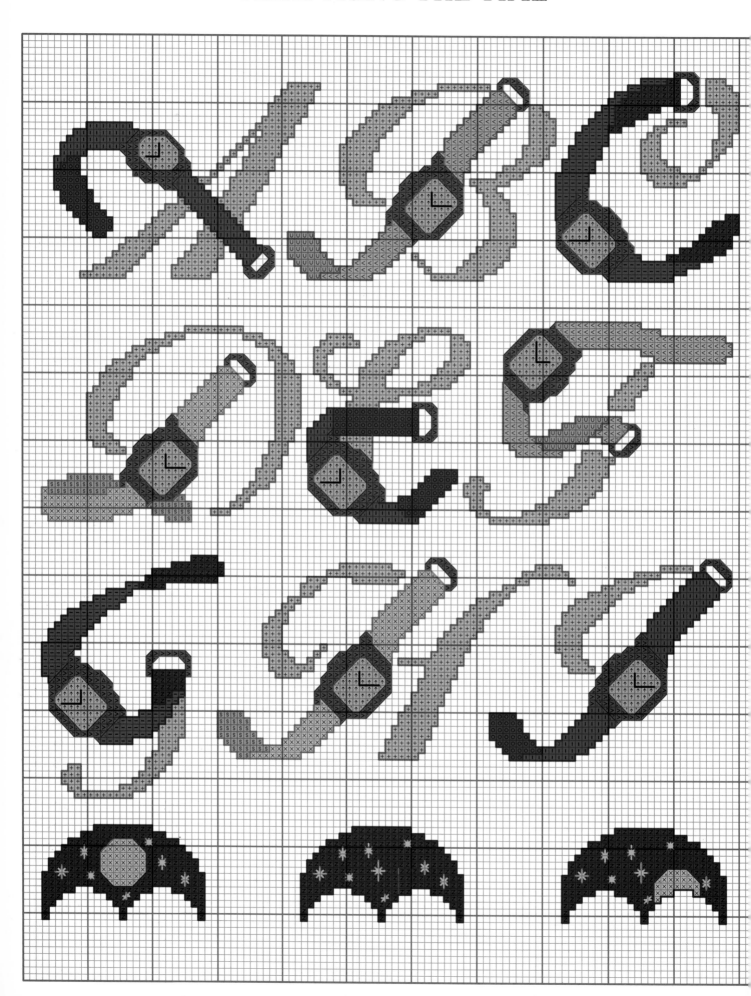

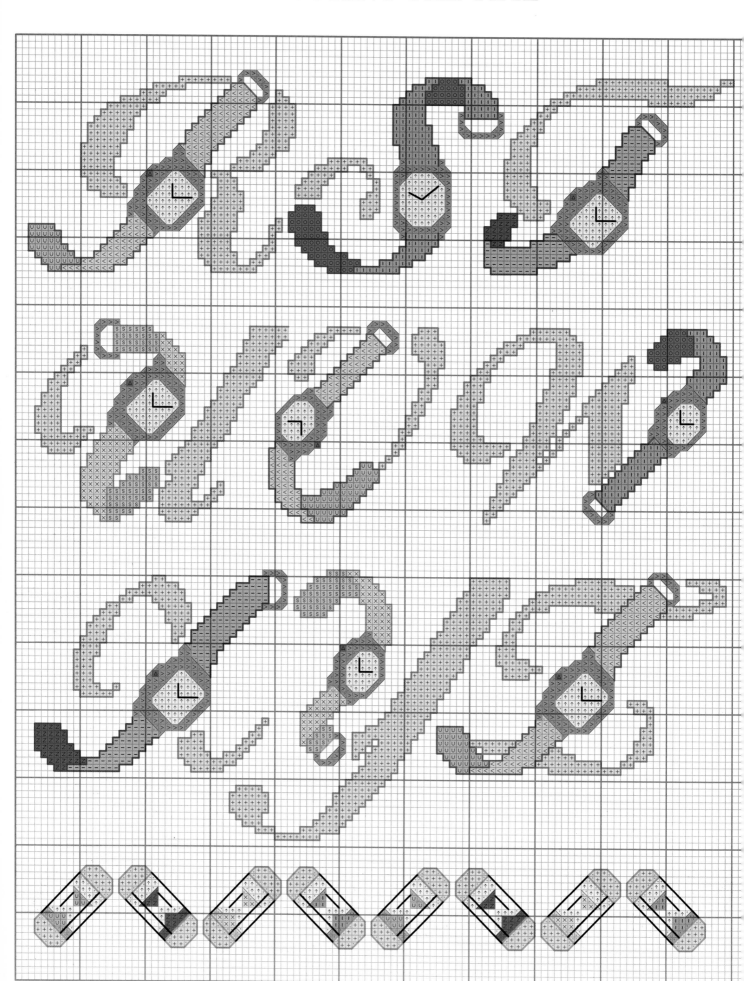

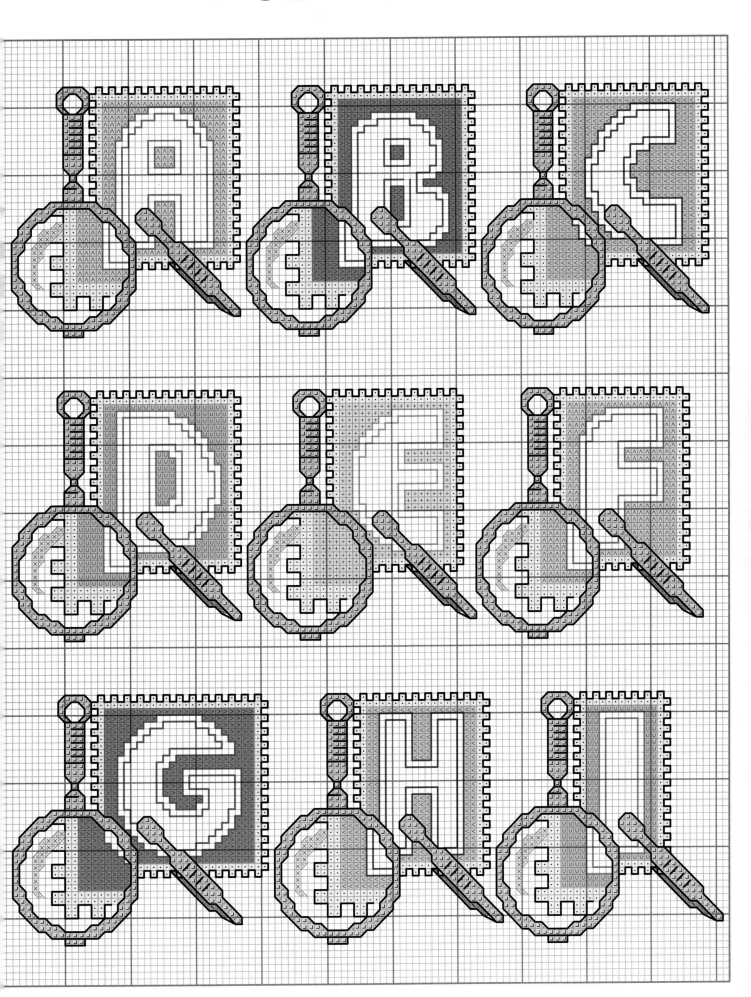

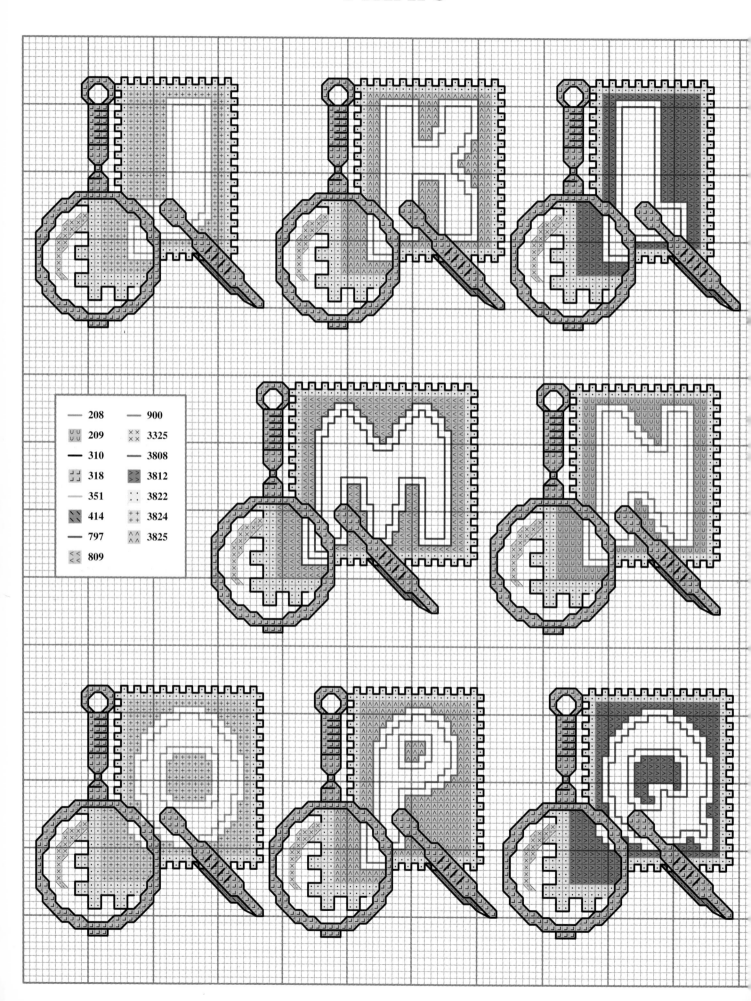

— 208	— 900
⊔⊔ 209	×× 3325
— 310	— 3808
⊔⊔ 318	◥◢ 3812
— 351	∴ 3822
◥◢ 414	++ 3824
— 797	∧∧ 3825
⟨⟨ 809	

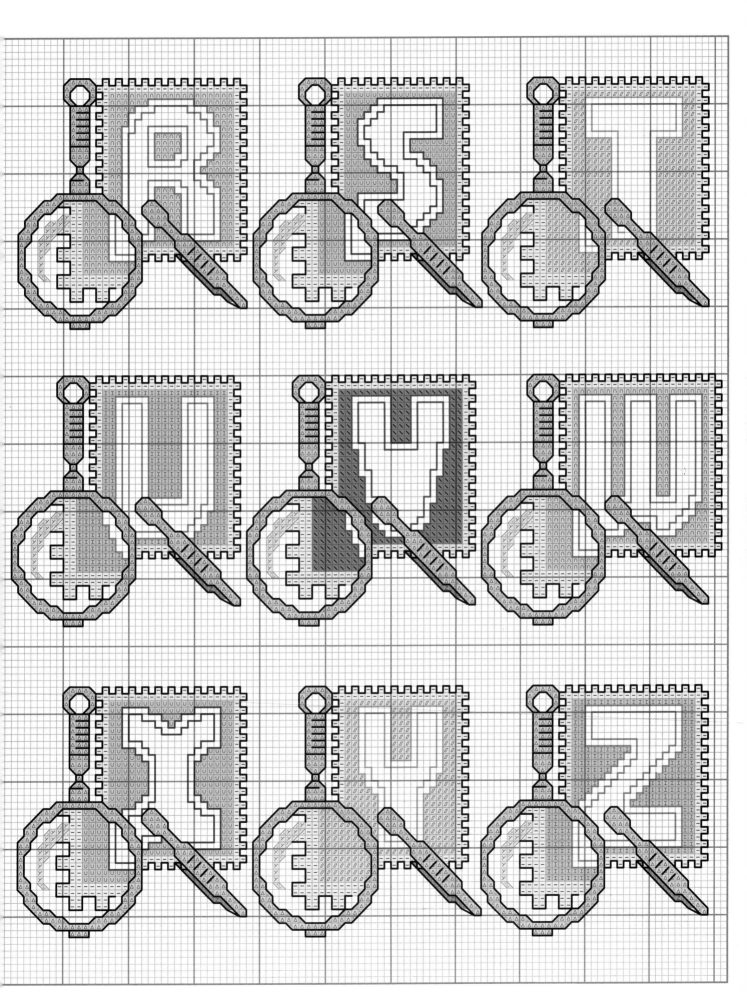

BASKETS

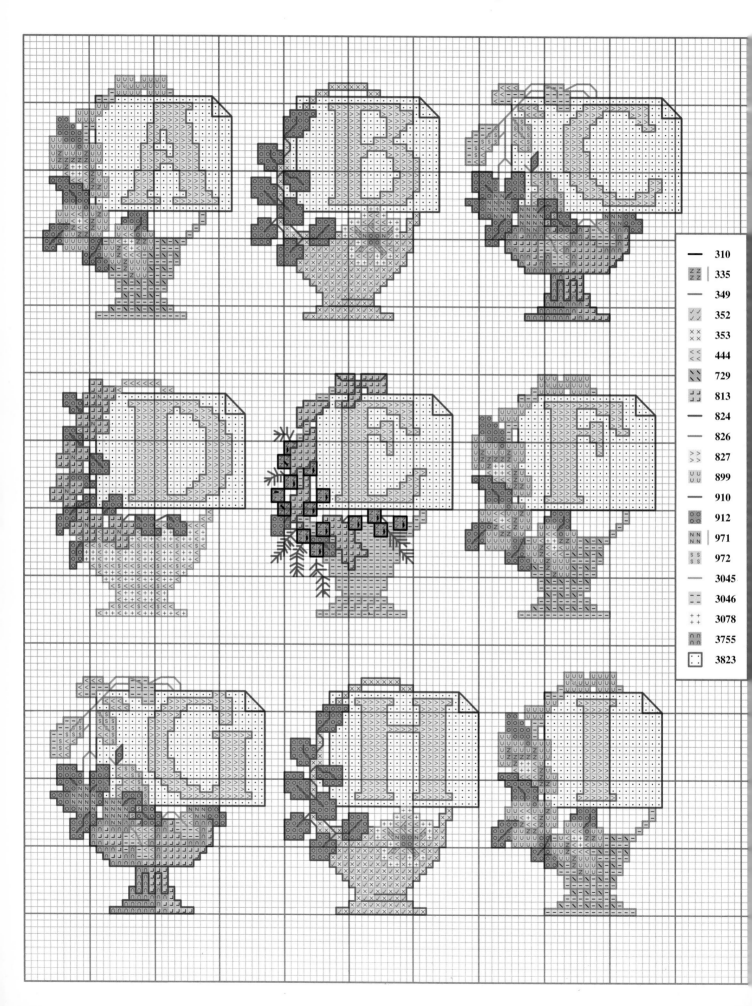

—	310
ZZ	335
—	349
✓✓	352
××	353
<<	444
＼＼	729
⌐⌐	813
—	824
—	826
>>	827
UU	899
—	910
OO	912
NN	971
SS	972
—	3045
⁻⁻	3046
++	3078
⌐⌐	3755
∴	3823

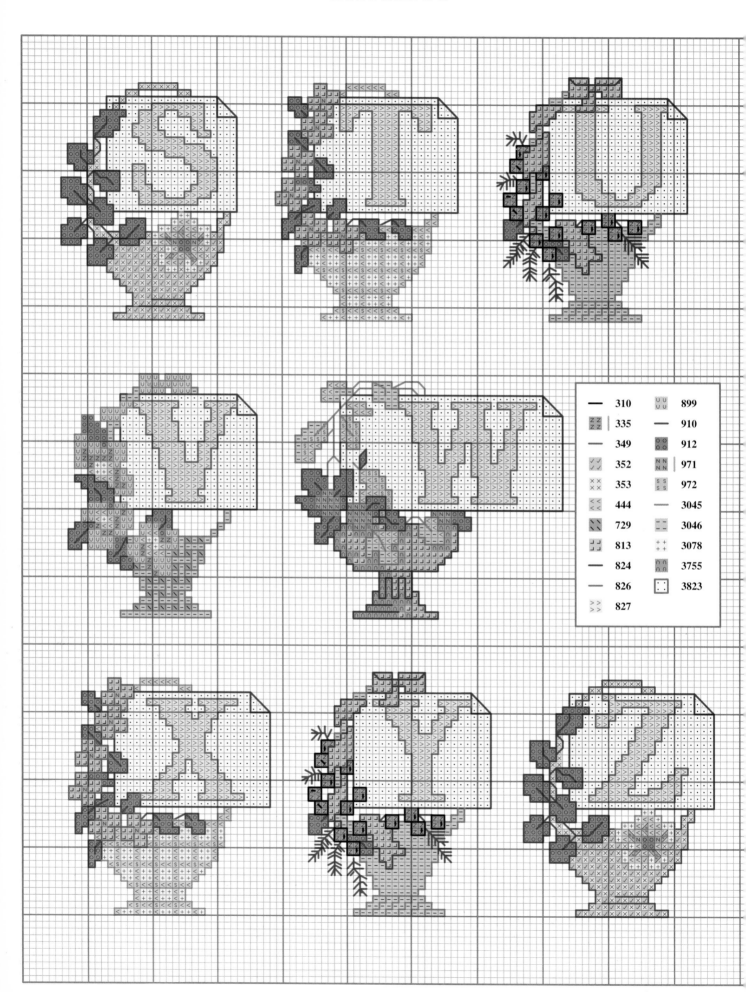

—	310	U U U	899
Z Z Z	335	—	910
—	349	O O	912
✓ ✓	352	N N N	971
X X	353	S S S	972
< <	444	—	3045
◥◣	729	- -	3046
◢◣	813	+ +	3078
—	824	◠◠	3755
—	826	⬚	3823
> >	827		

GRAPE HARVEST

CAPTAIN'S CAP

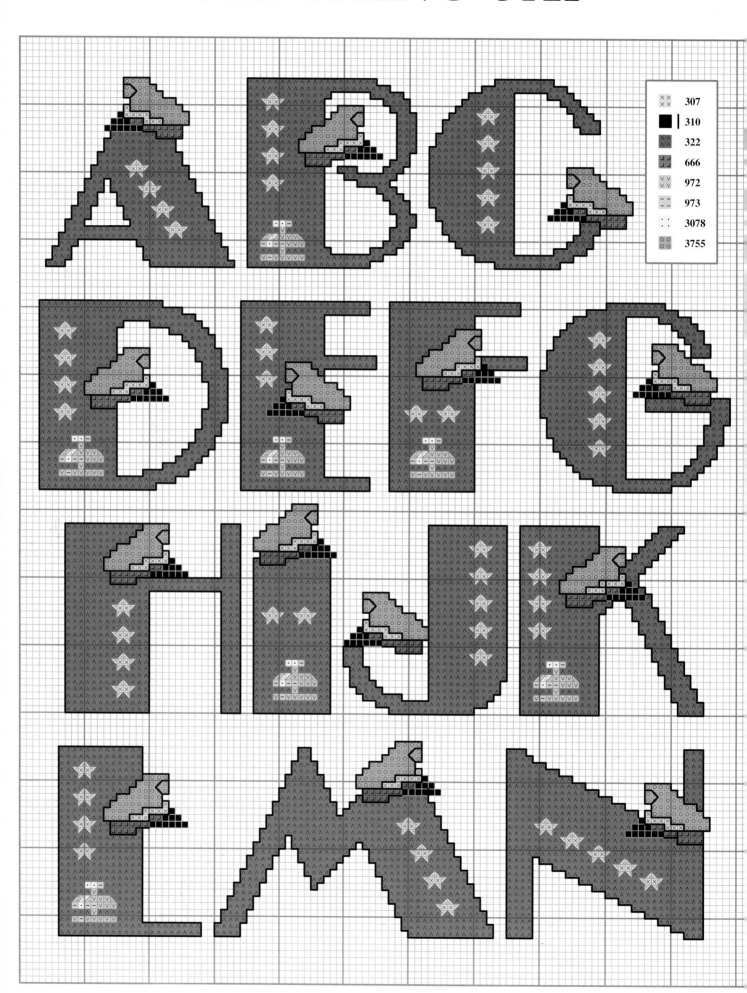

✕✕ ✕✕	307
⬛ |	310
▲▲	322
⊞⊞	666
∨∨ ∨∨	972
−− −−	973
∶∶	3078
�◌ ◌◌	3755

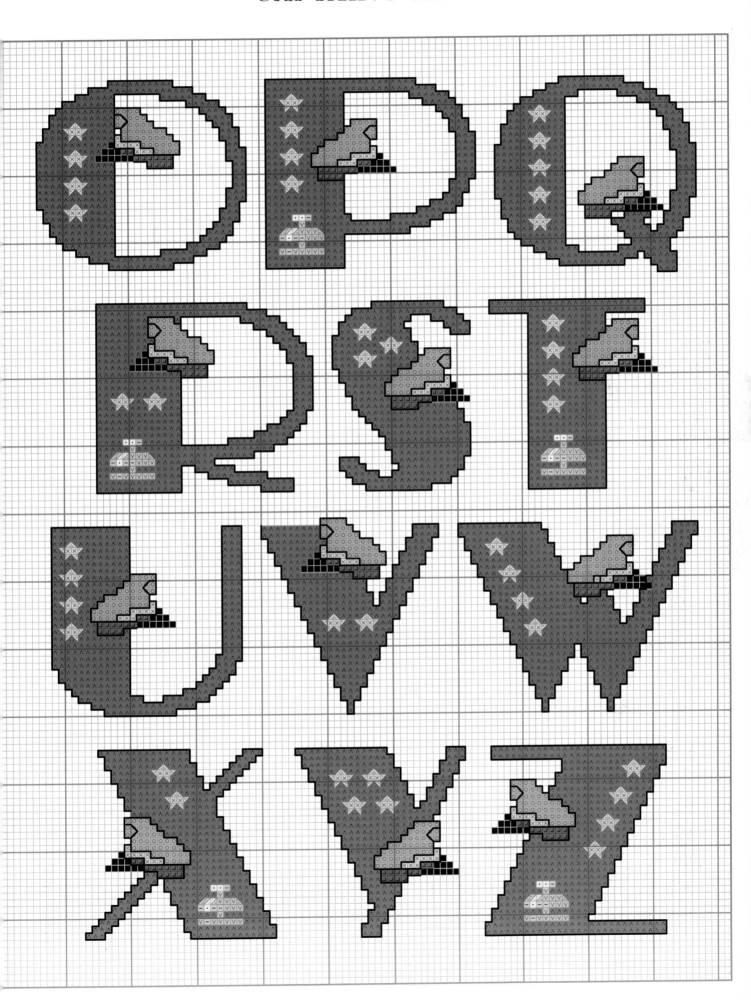

WINDSURFING

—	310
▼▼	312
⁴⁴	340
++	353
→→	444
--	519
◣◣	553
◳◳	606
××	725
׀׀	742
∩∩	783
⌐⌐	798
ˢˢ	799
••	814
○○	947
ᴛᴛ	975
ɴɴ	3607
<<	3608
∪∪	3755
ℤℤ	3760
↑↑	3761

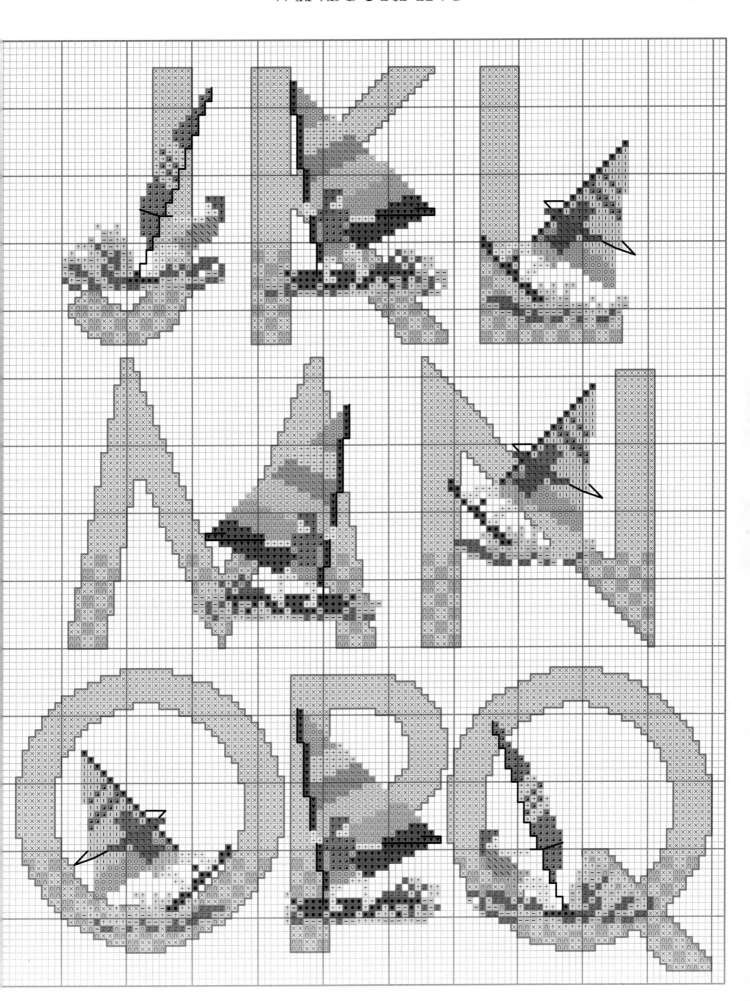

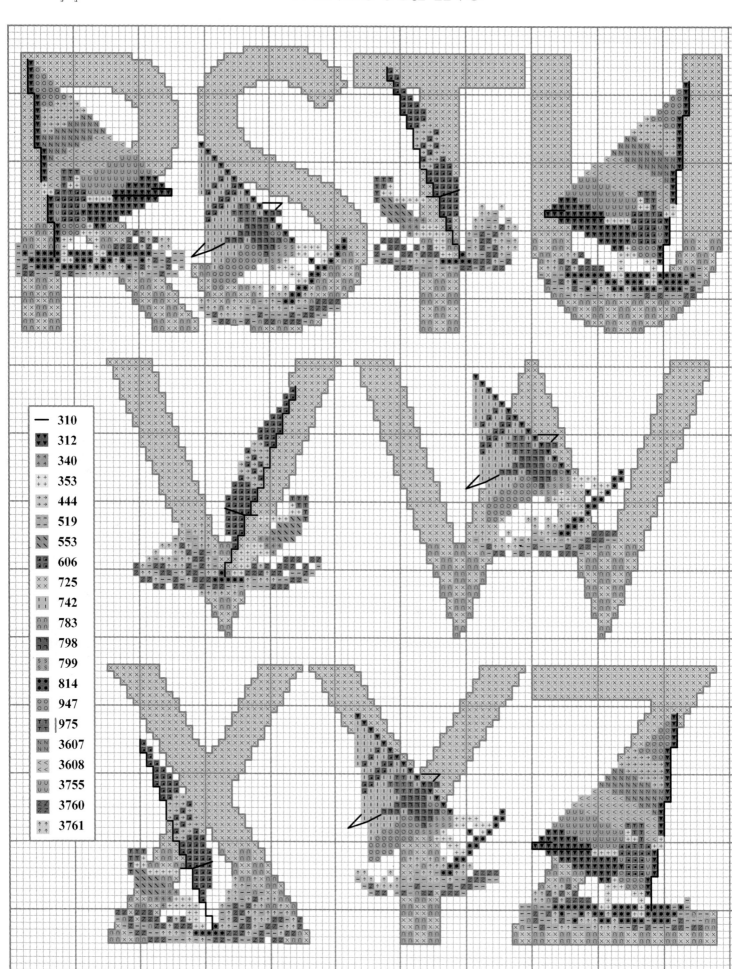

FROM THE EAST

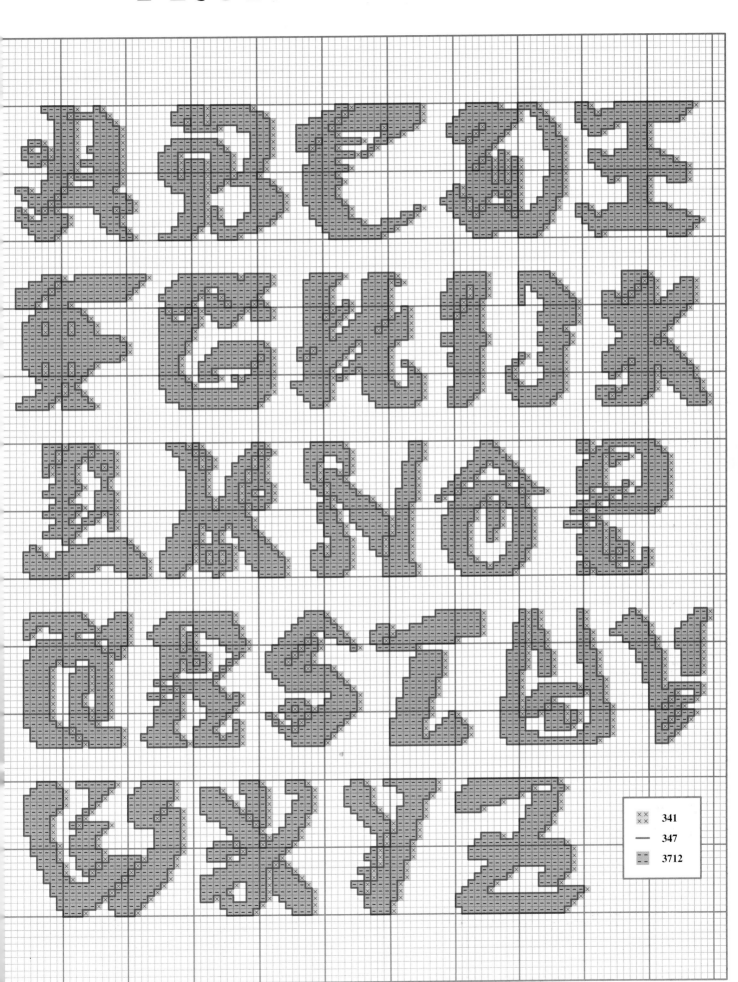

××	341
—	347
▦	3712

ART NOUVEAU STYLE

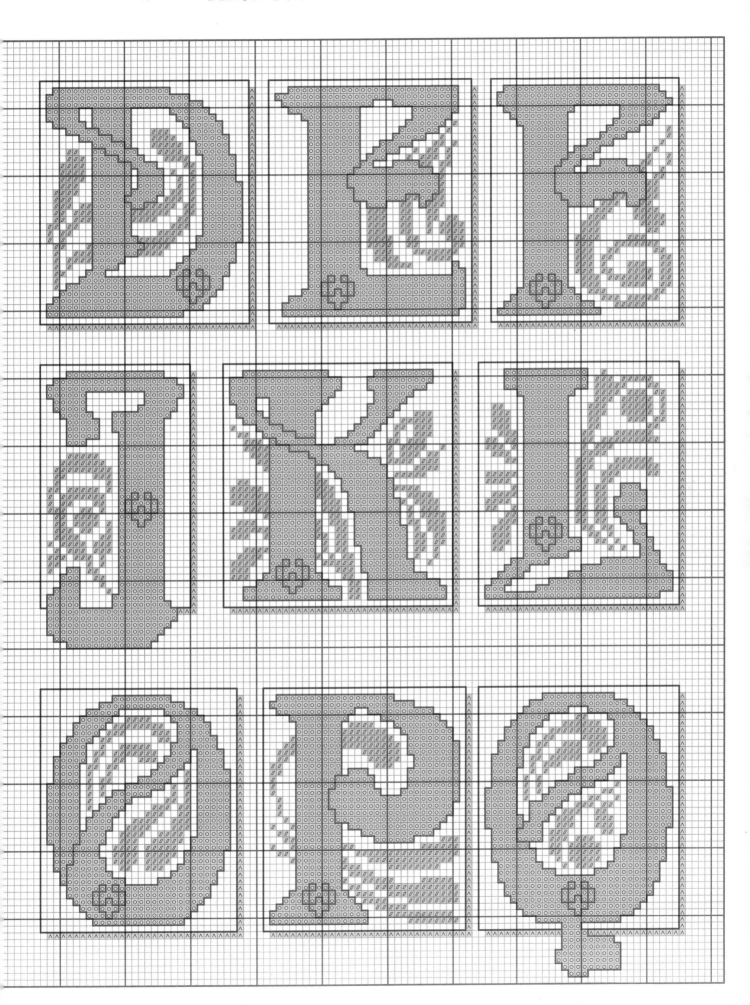

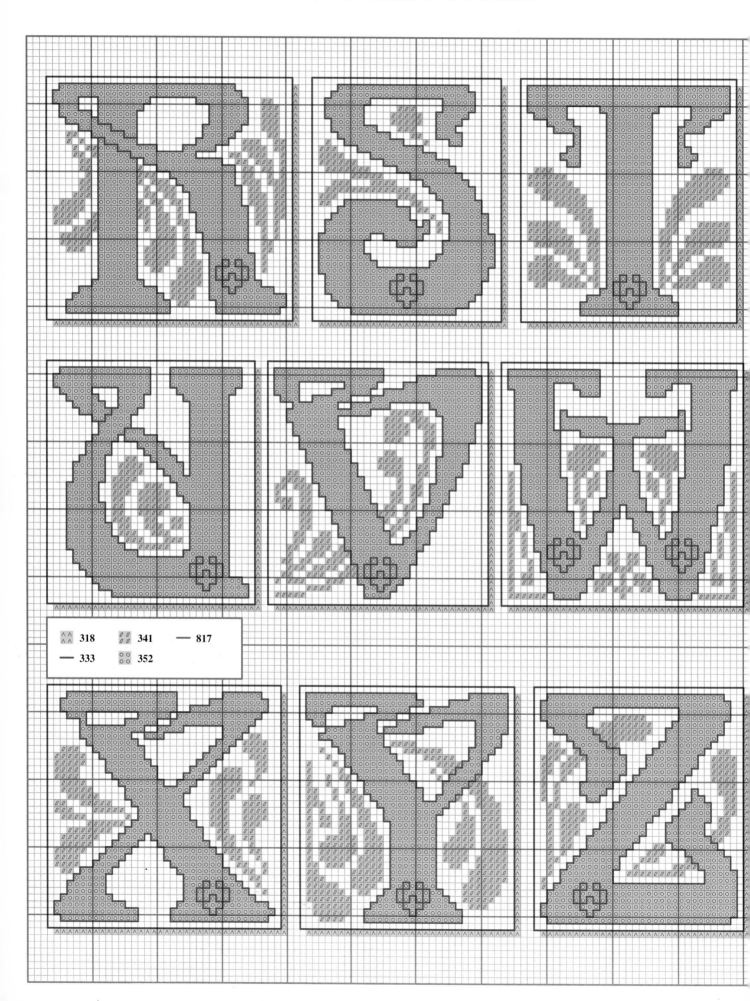

| ^^ ^^ | 318 | oo oo | 341 | — | 817 |
| — | 333 | oo oo | 352 | | |

■	310	++ ++	754
—	349	▨	792
▨	350	—	900
^^	352	—	909
--	444	◉◉	911
UU	742	◁◁	932
⬚	745	××	3752

∧∧	347
++	353
○○	435
:=	436
<<	437
××	444
■	801
—	817
—	904
►►	906
Z Z	931
∪∪	971
⬚	3078

	310		676
	312		762
	334	—	900
	351	—	904
	352		906
	353		907
	415		3755
	444		3820
	666		3822

OLIVES

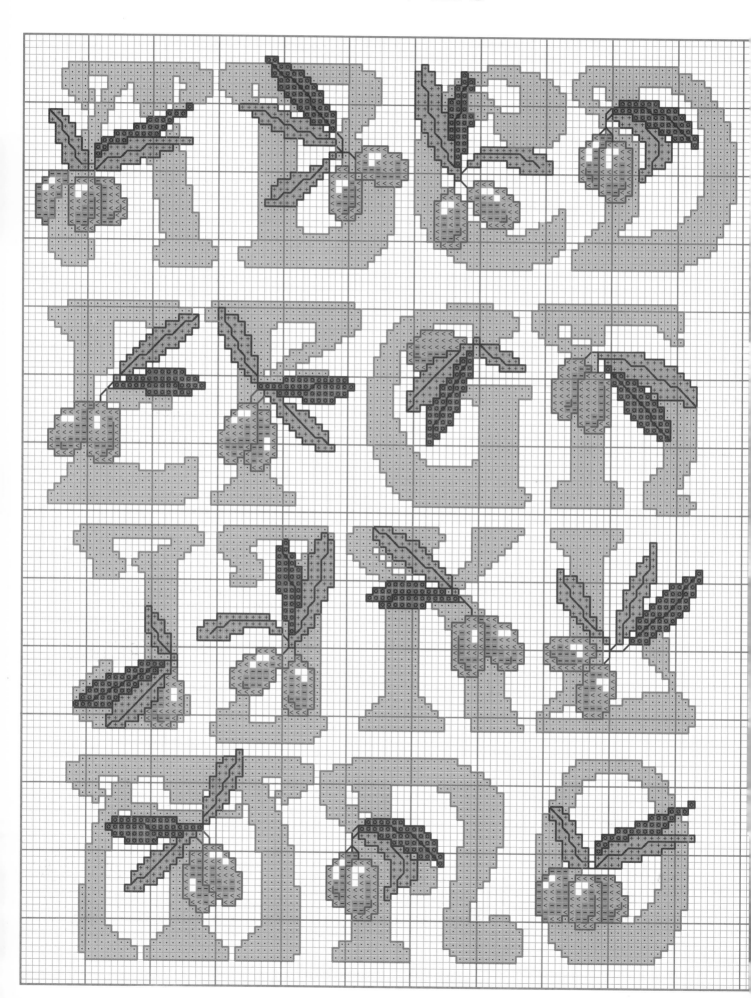

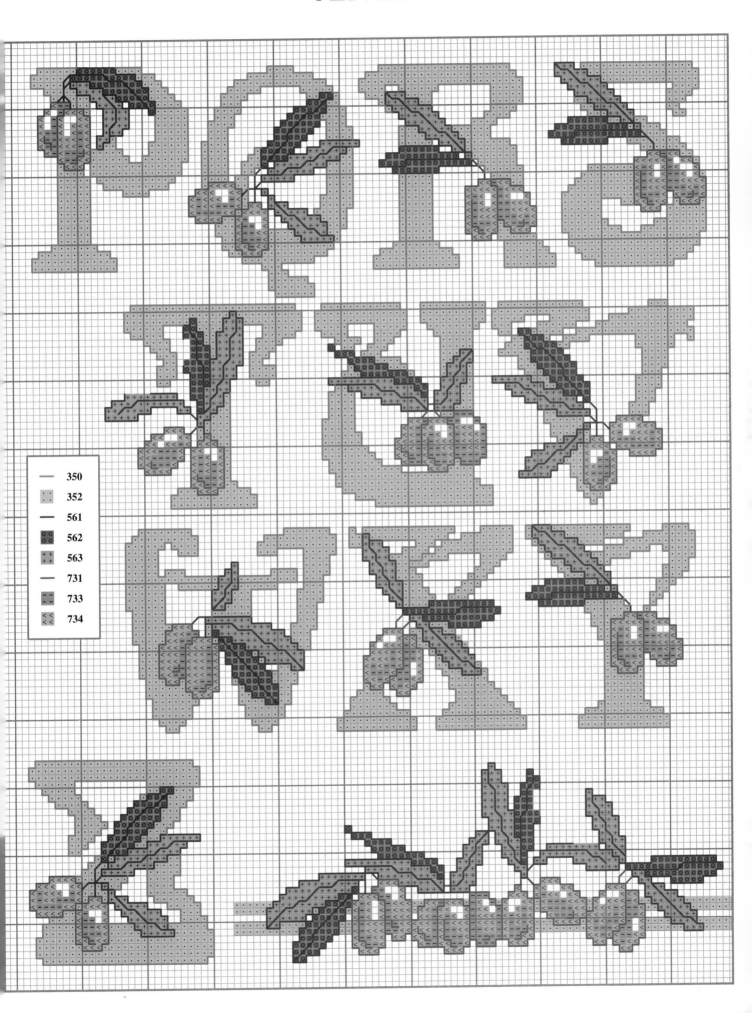

——	350
⫶	352
——	561
◐◐	562
＋＋	563
——	731
▬▬	733
⋖⋖	734

	310		523		734
	318		524		738
	321		550		740
	350		552		742
	352		553		743
	356		561		744
	413		562		745
	414		563		762
	435		666		791
	436		699		815
	437		701		900
	470		703		948
	471		731		
	472		733		

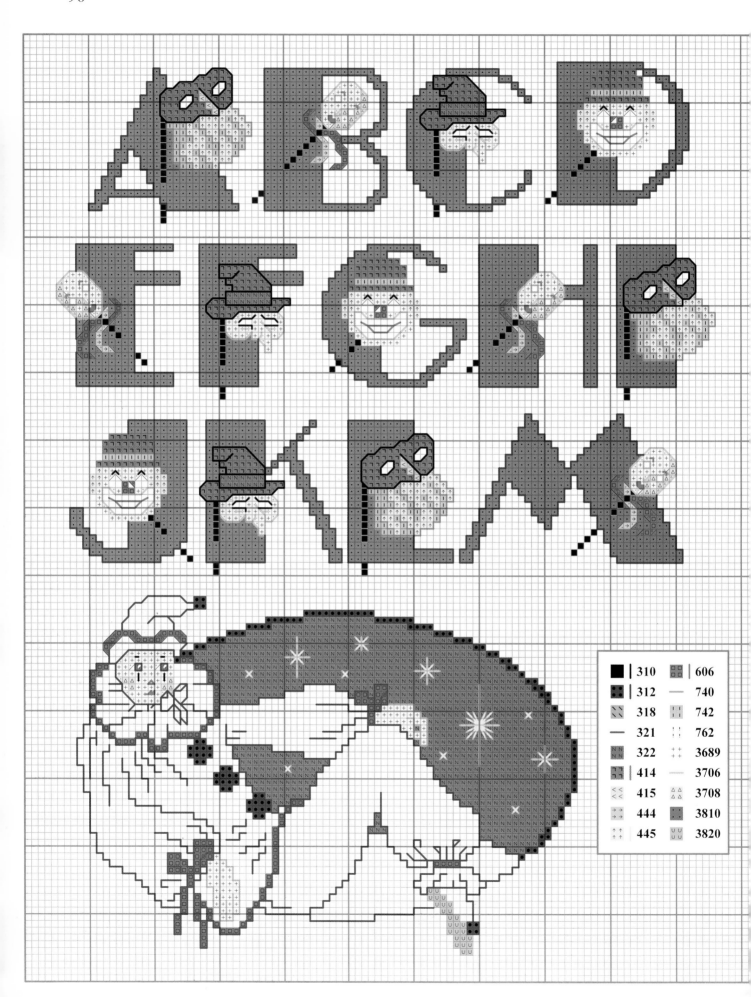

	310		606
	312	—	740
	318		742
—	321		762
N	322	+ +	3689
	414		3706
< <	415	△ △	3708
→	444		3810
↑ ↑	445	U U	3820

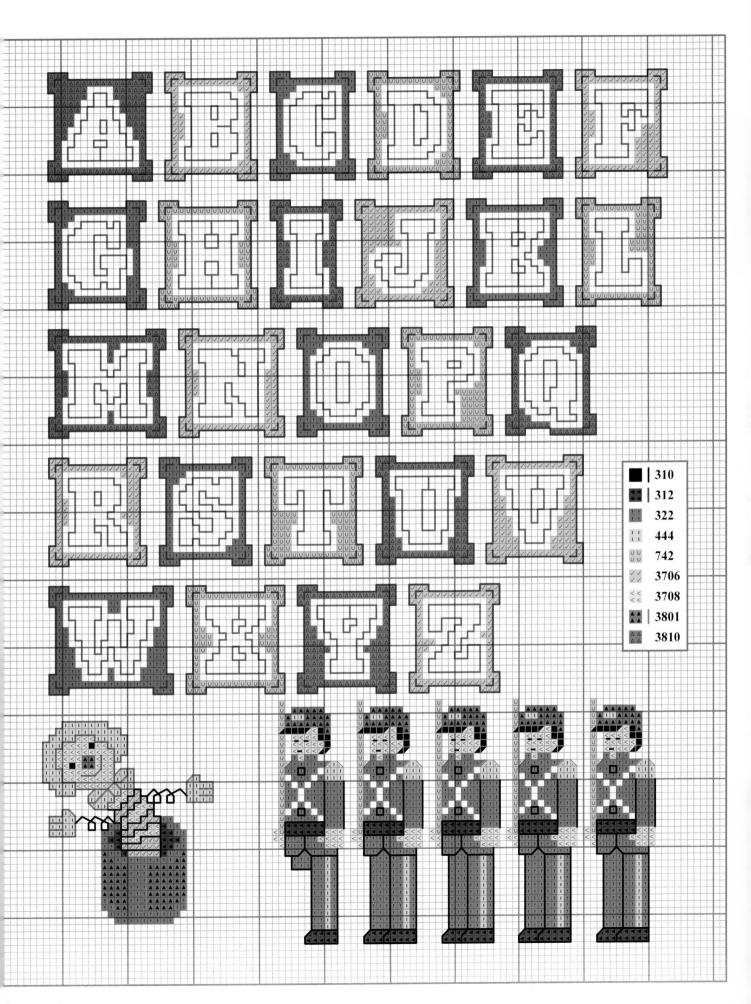

AMERICAN FLAG

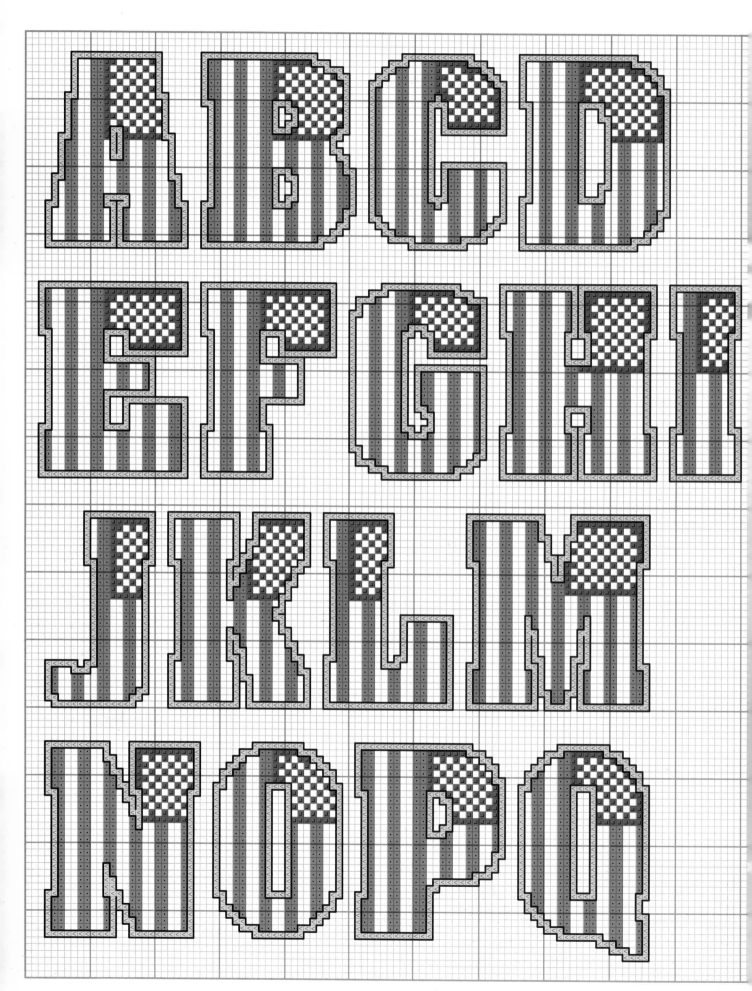

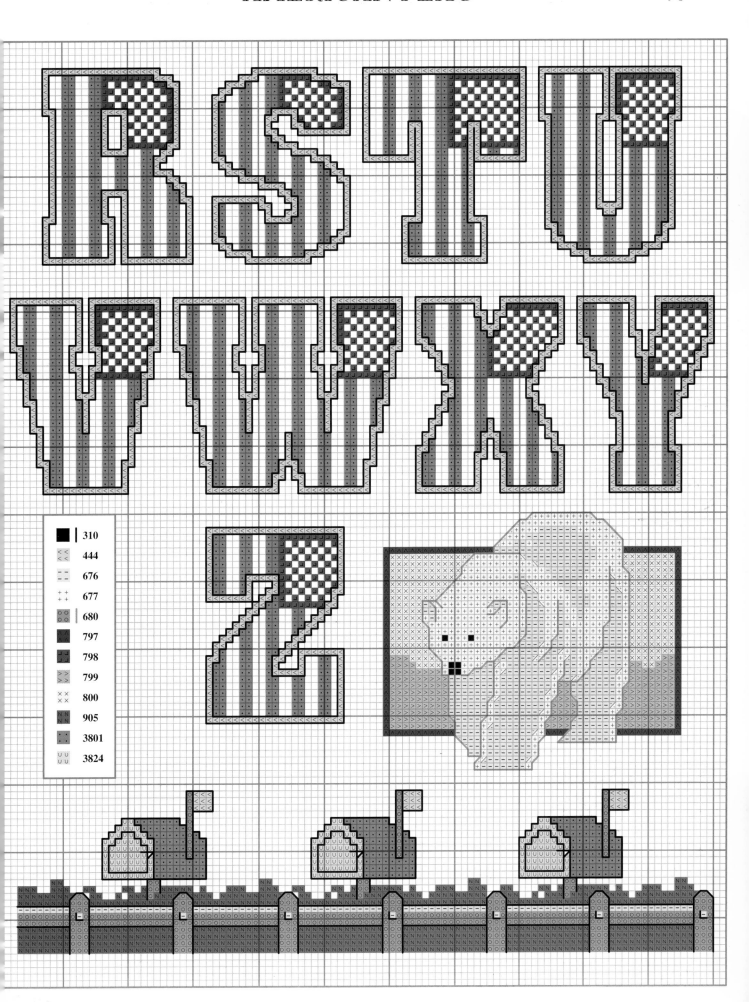

TOYS

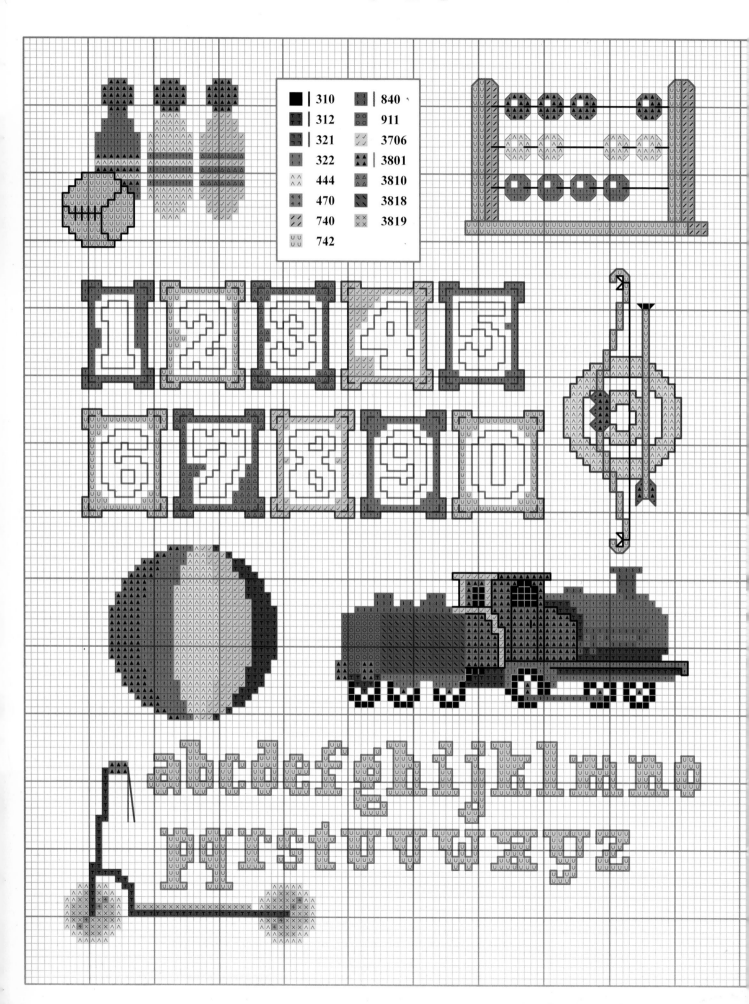

■	310	▮	840
▮	312	◌	911
▮	321	✓	3706
▮	322	▲	3801
^	444	▲	3810
◢	470	◥	3818
⁄	740	✕	3819
∪	742		